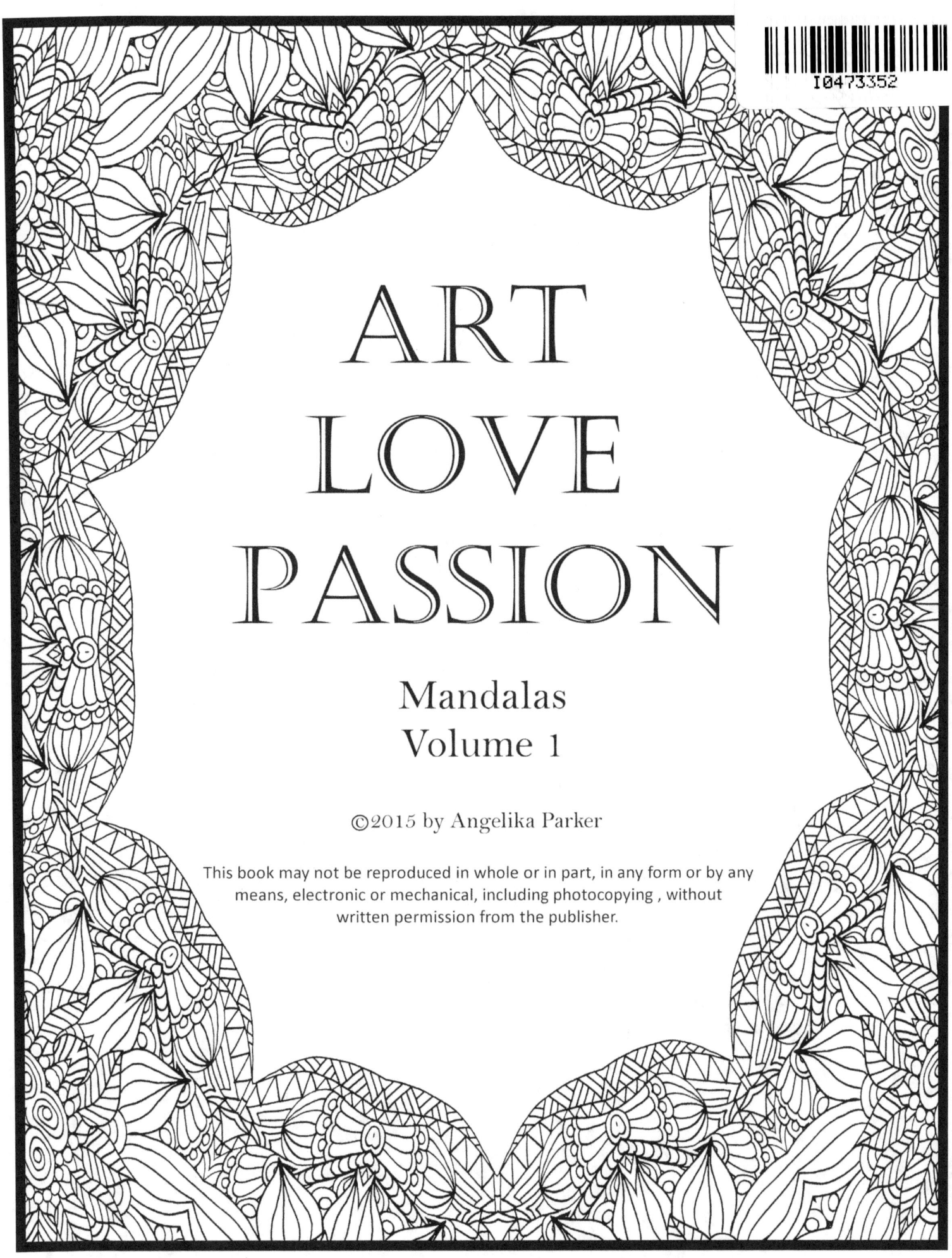

ART LOVE PASSION

Mandalas
Volume 1

©2015 by Angelika Parker

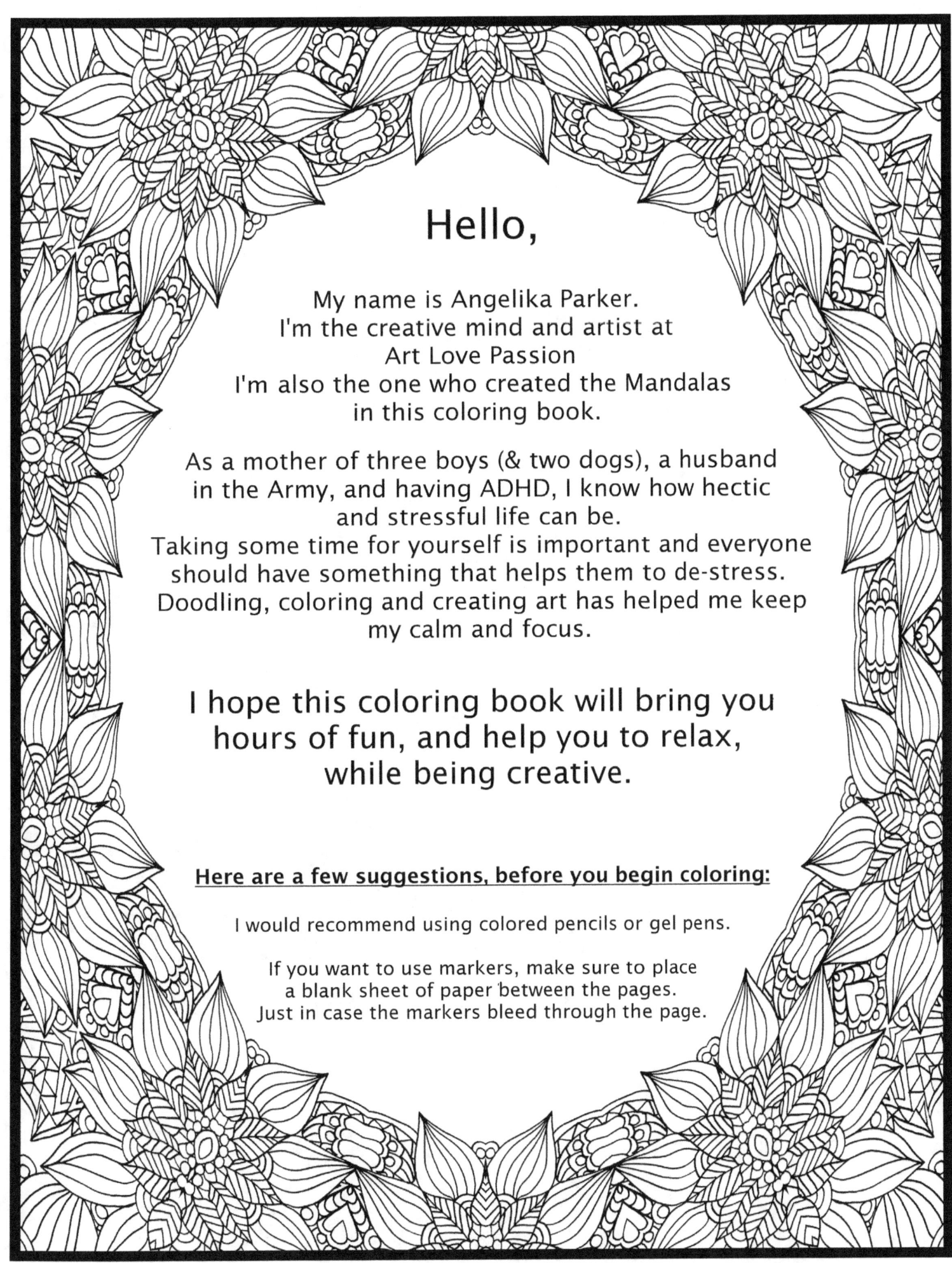

Hello,

My name is Angelika Parker.
I'm the creative mind and artist at
Art Love Passion
I'm also the one who created the Mandalas
in this coloring book.

As a mother of three boys (& two dogs), a husband
in the Army, and having ADHD, I know how hectic
and stressful life can be.
Taking some time for yourself is important and everyone
should have something that helps them to de-stress.
Doodling, coloring and creating art has helped me keep
my calm and focus.

I hope this coloring book will bring you
hours of fun, and help you to relax,
while being creative.

Here are a few suggestions, before you begin coloring:

I would recommend using colored pencils or gel pens.

If you want to use markers, make sure to place
a blank sheet of paper between the pages.
Just in case the markers bleed through the page.

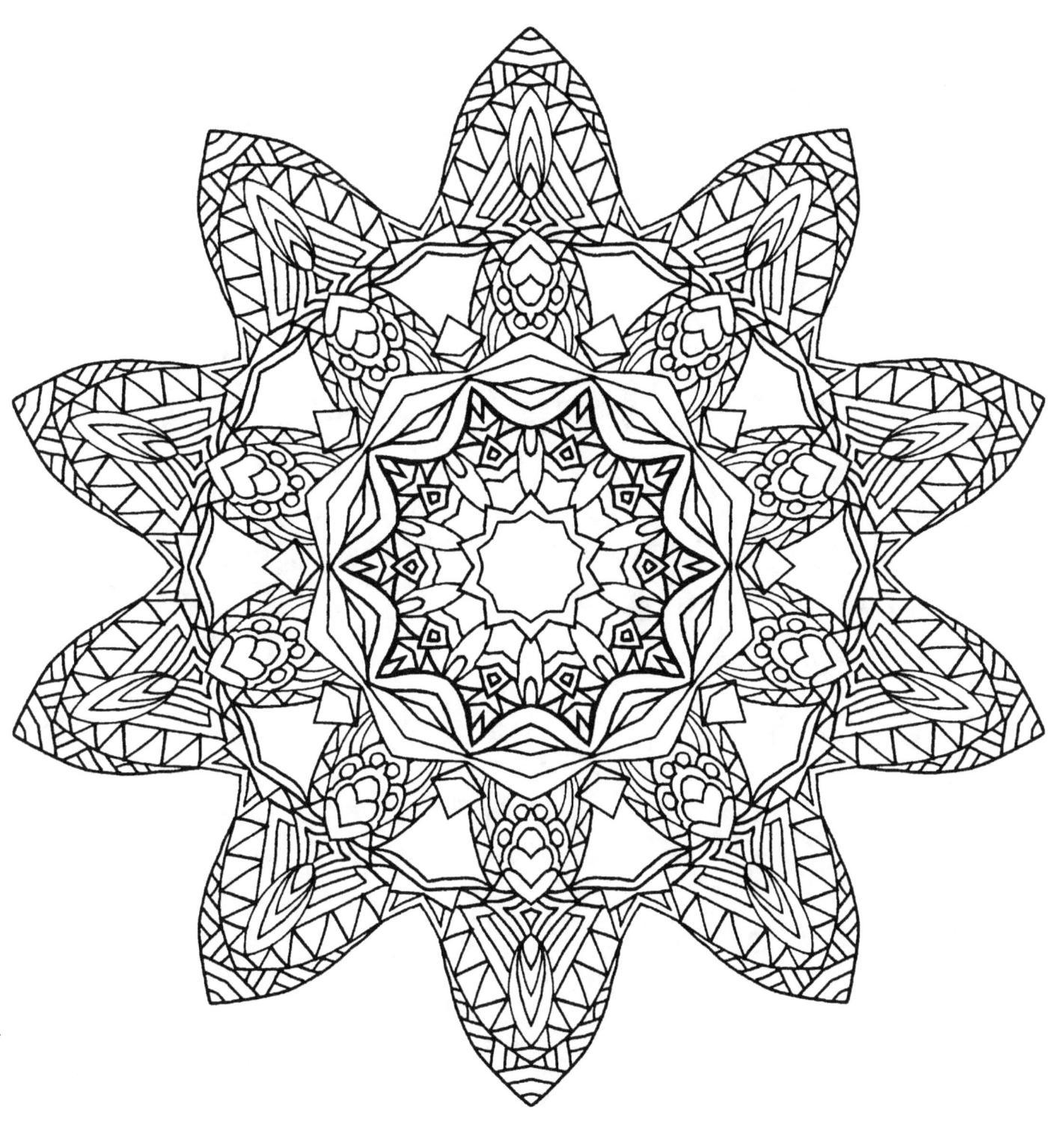

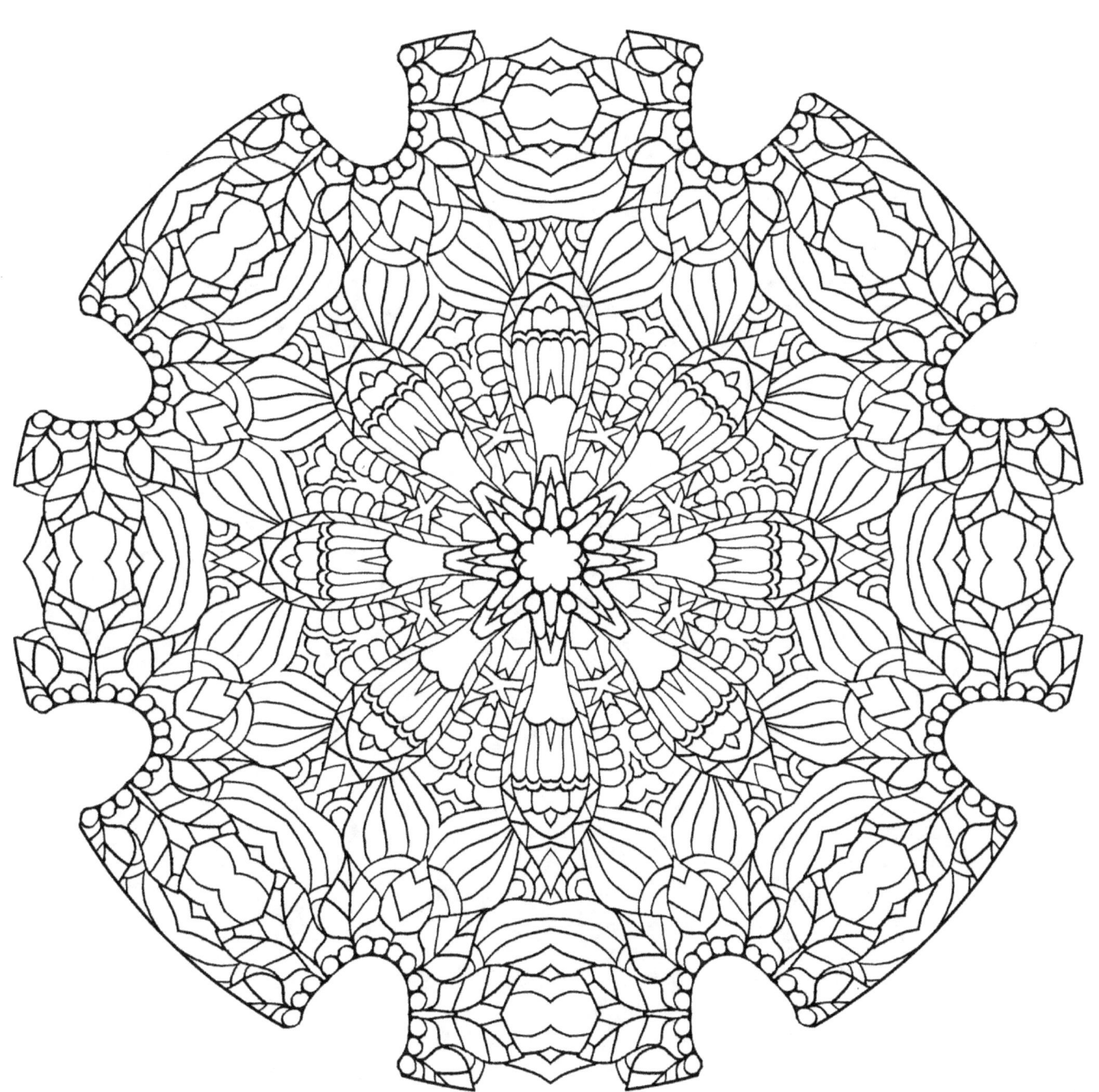

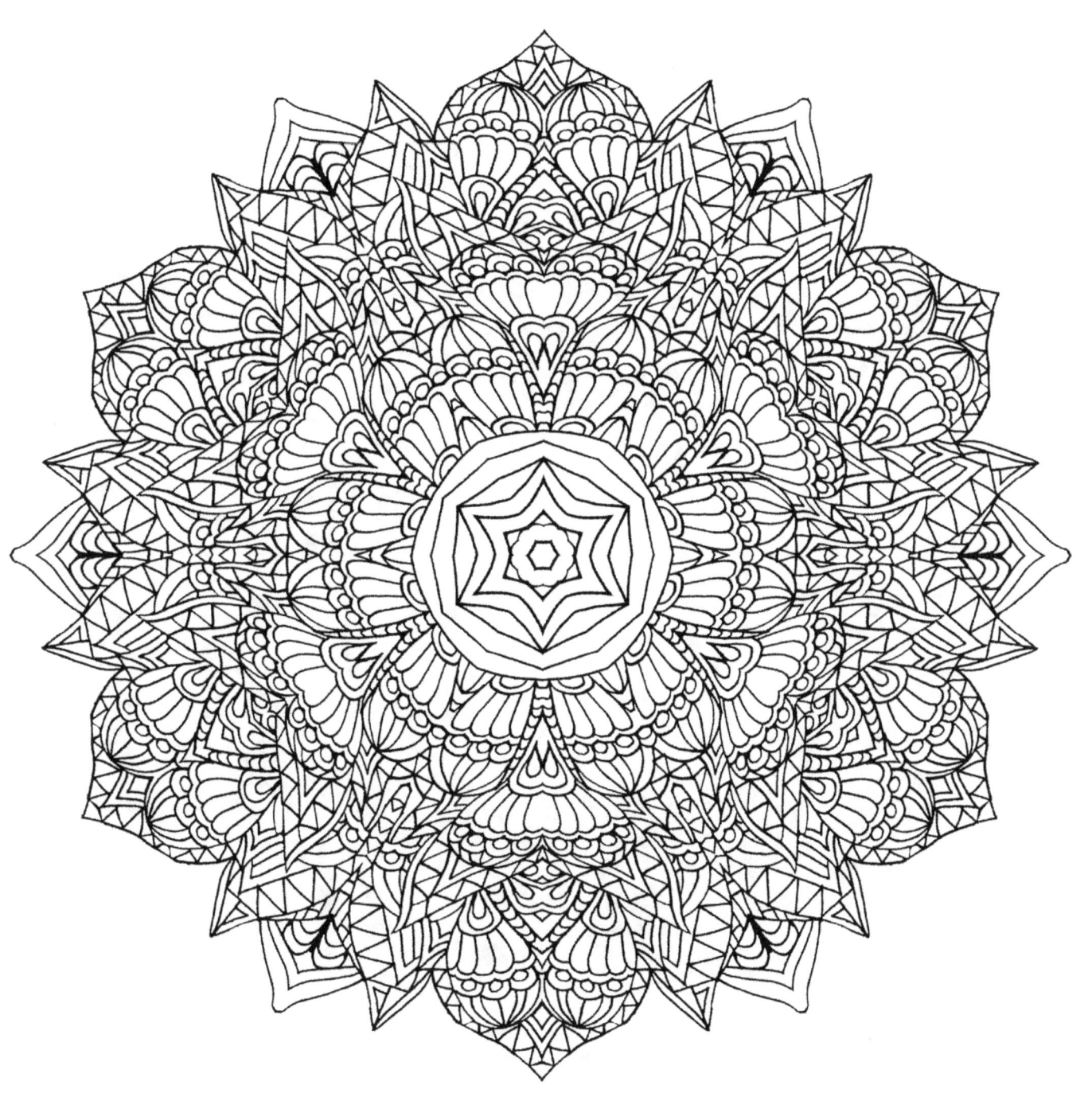

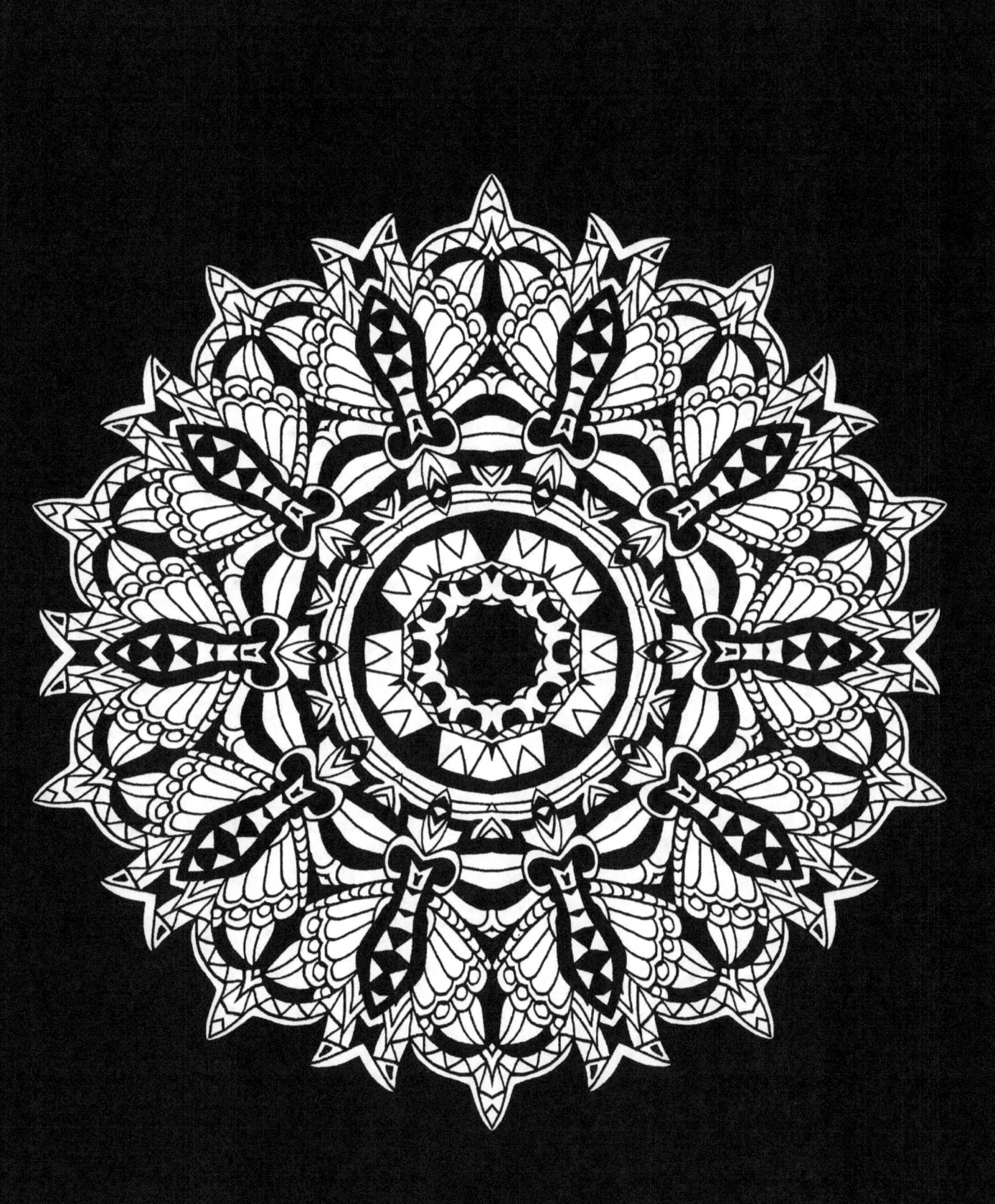

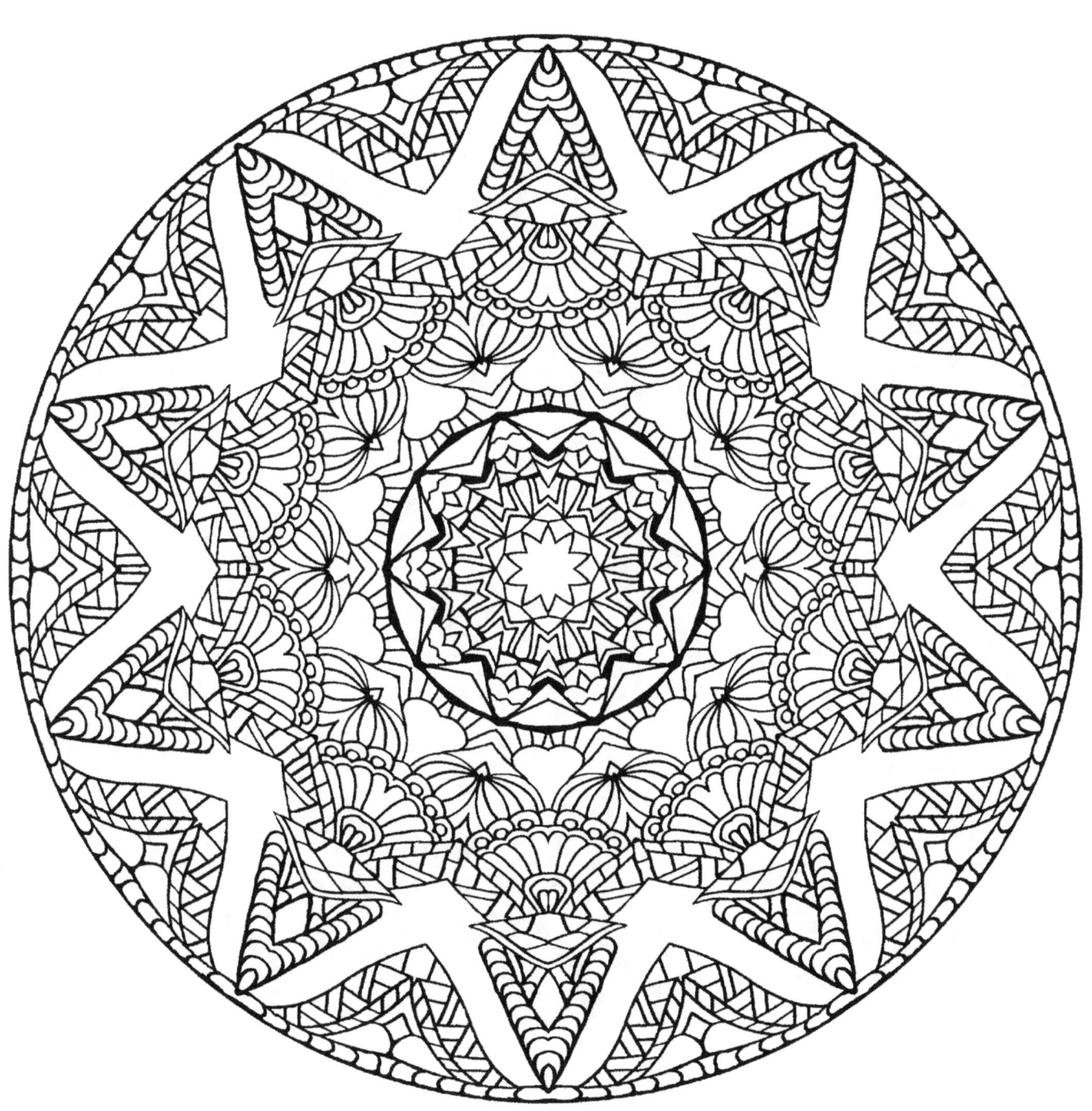

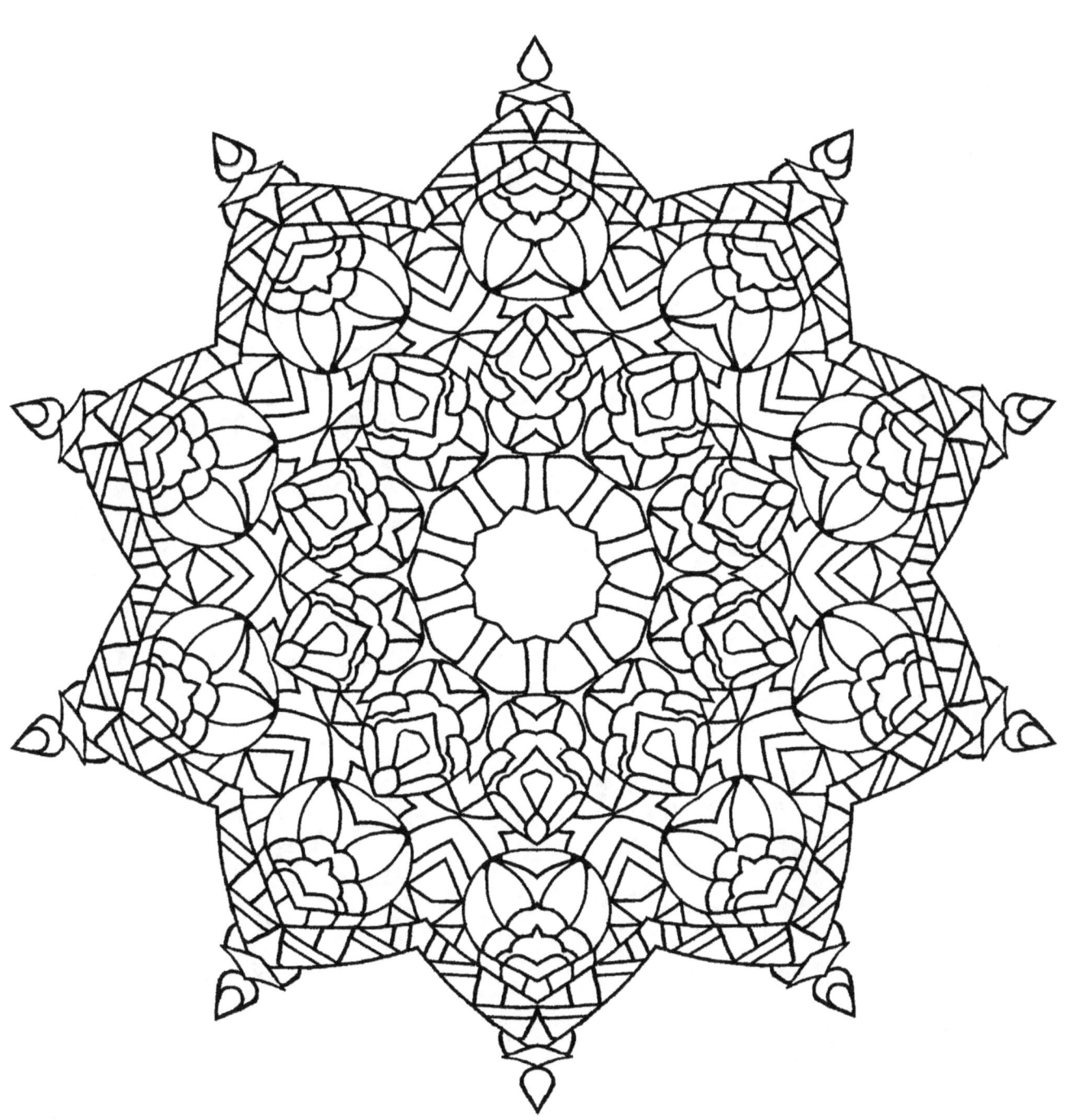

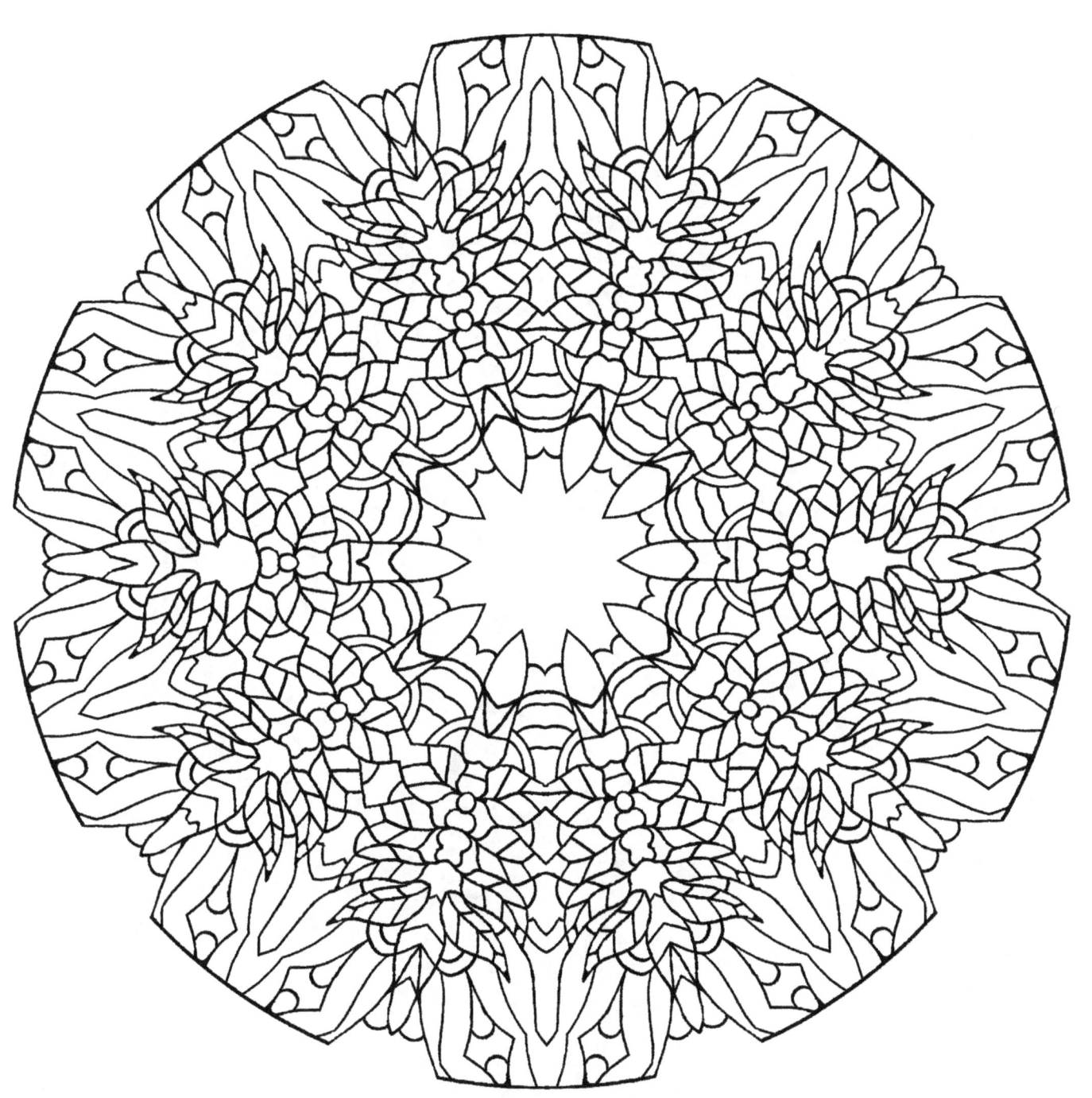

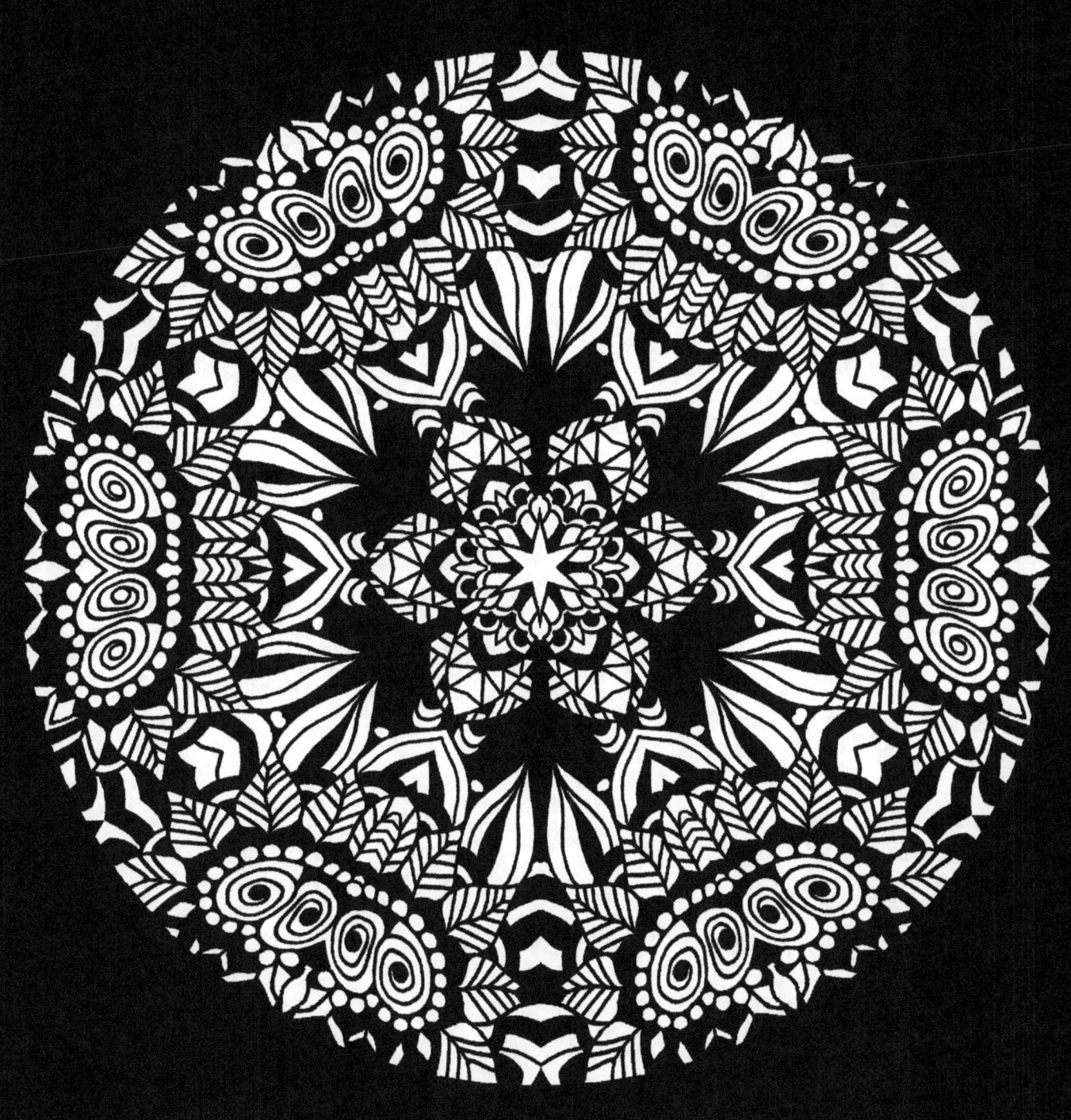

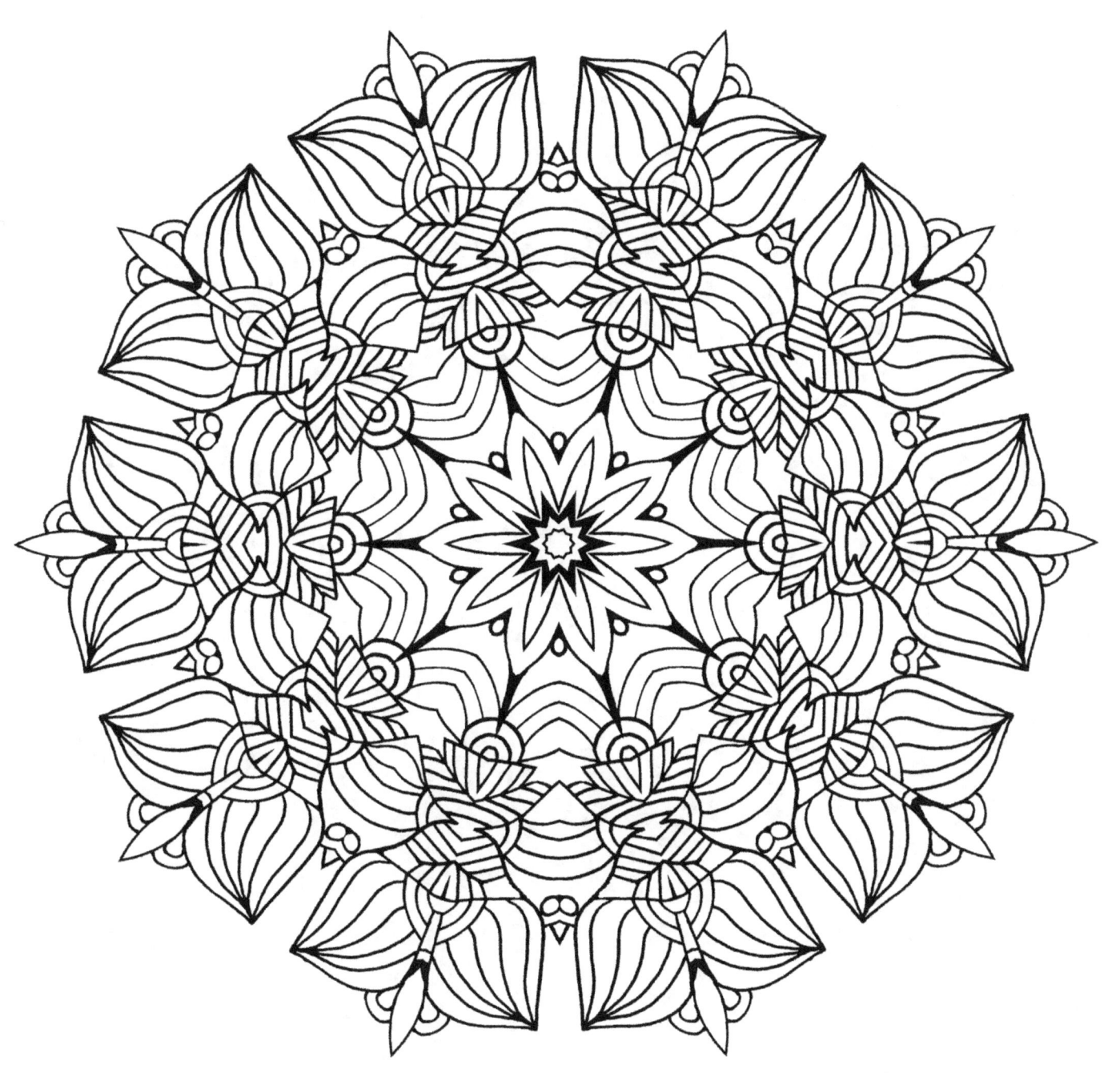

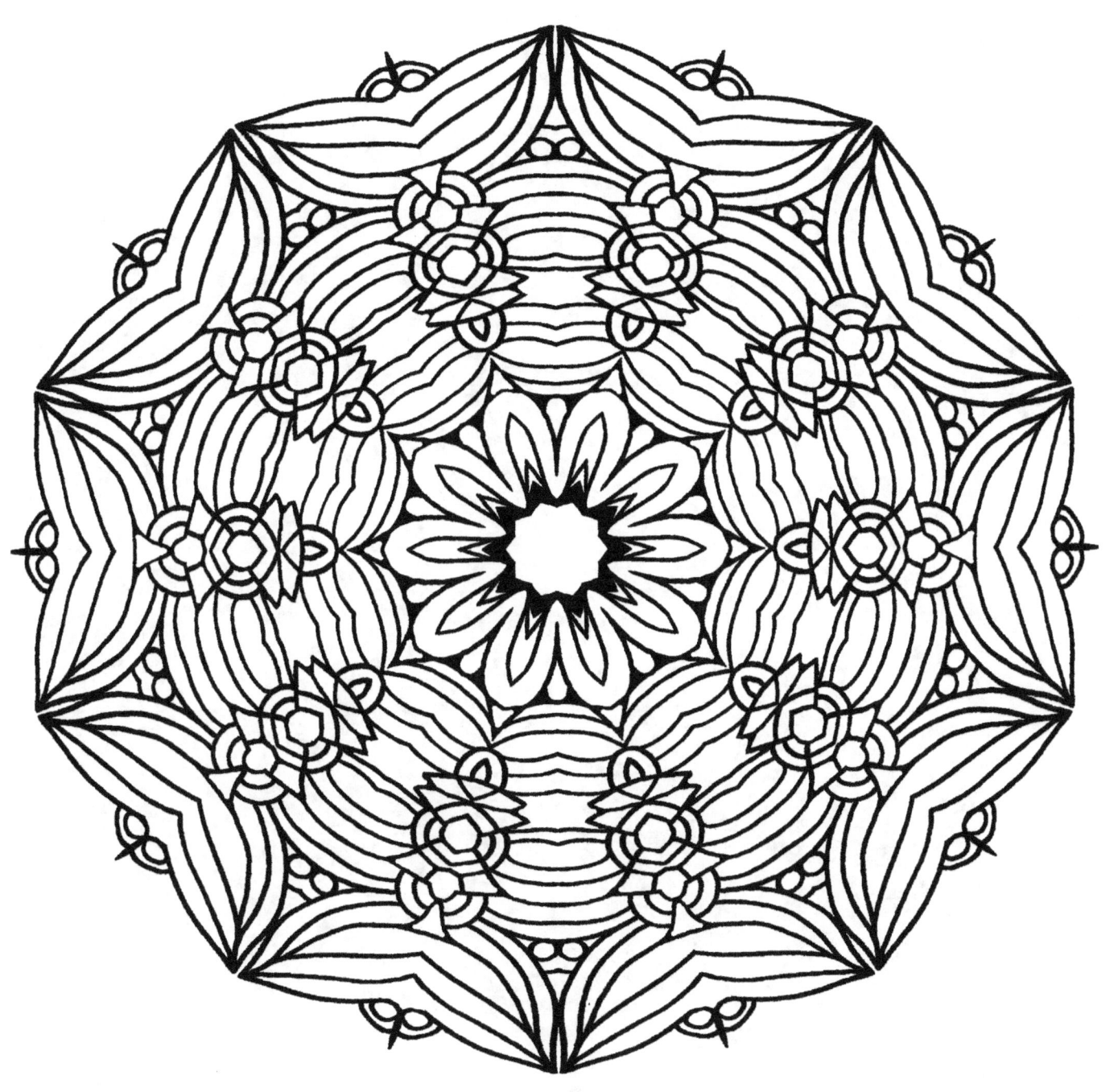

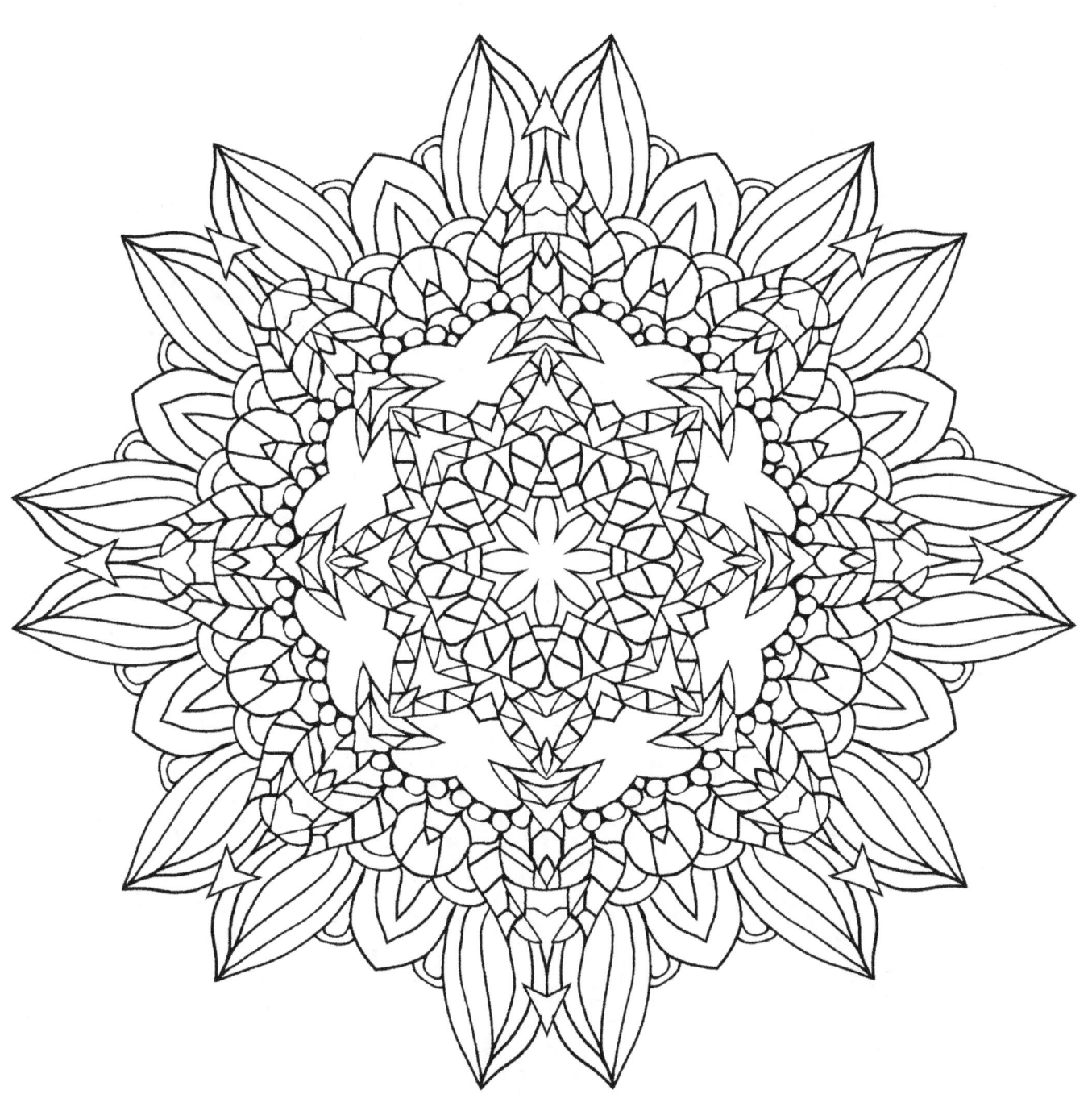

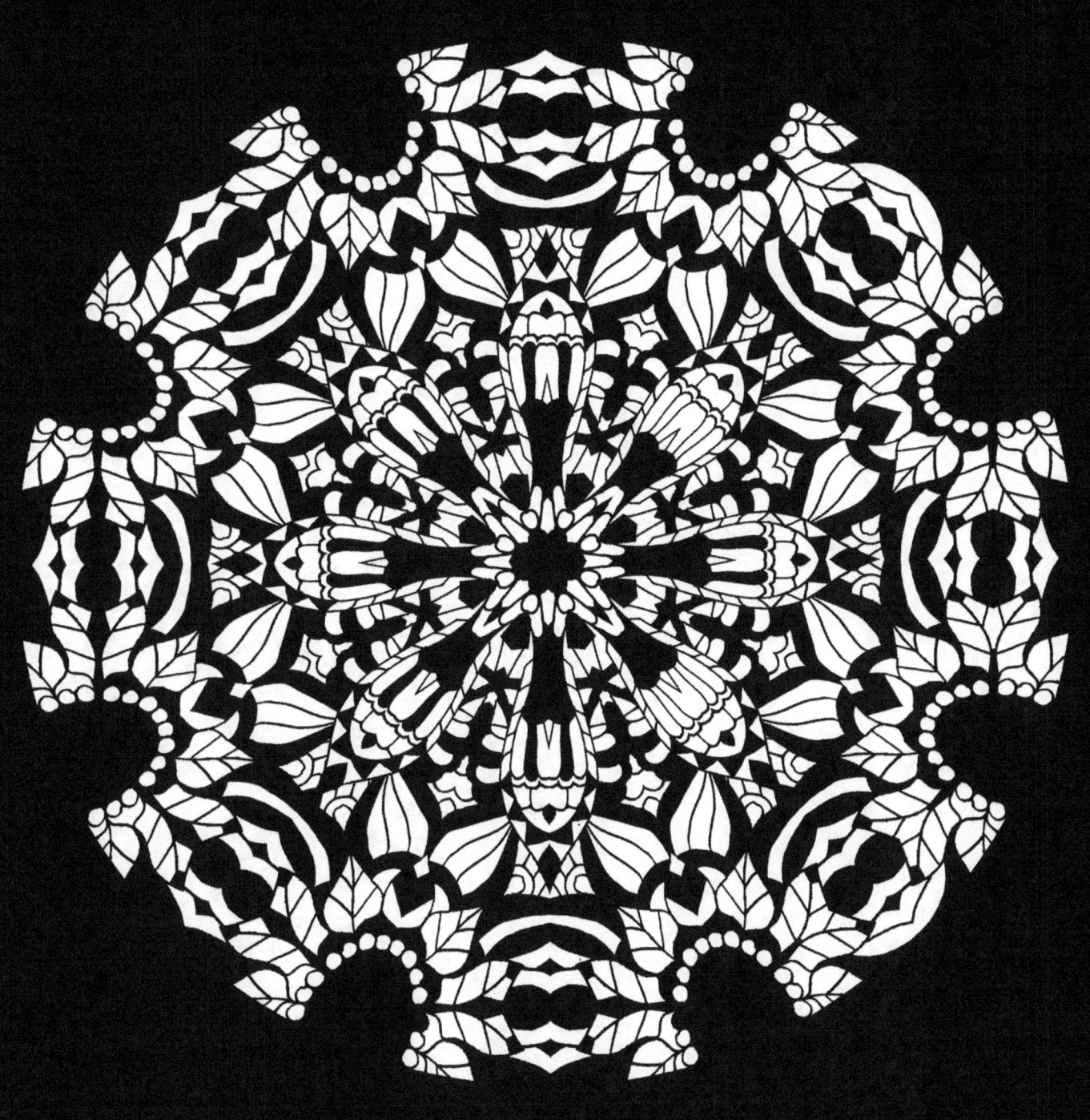

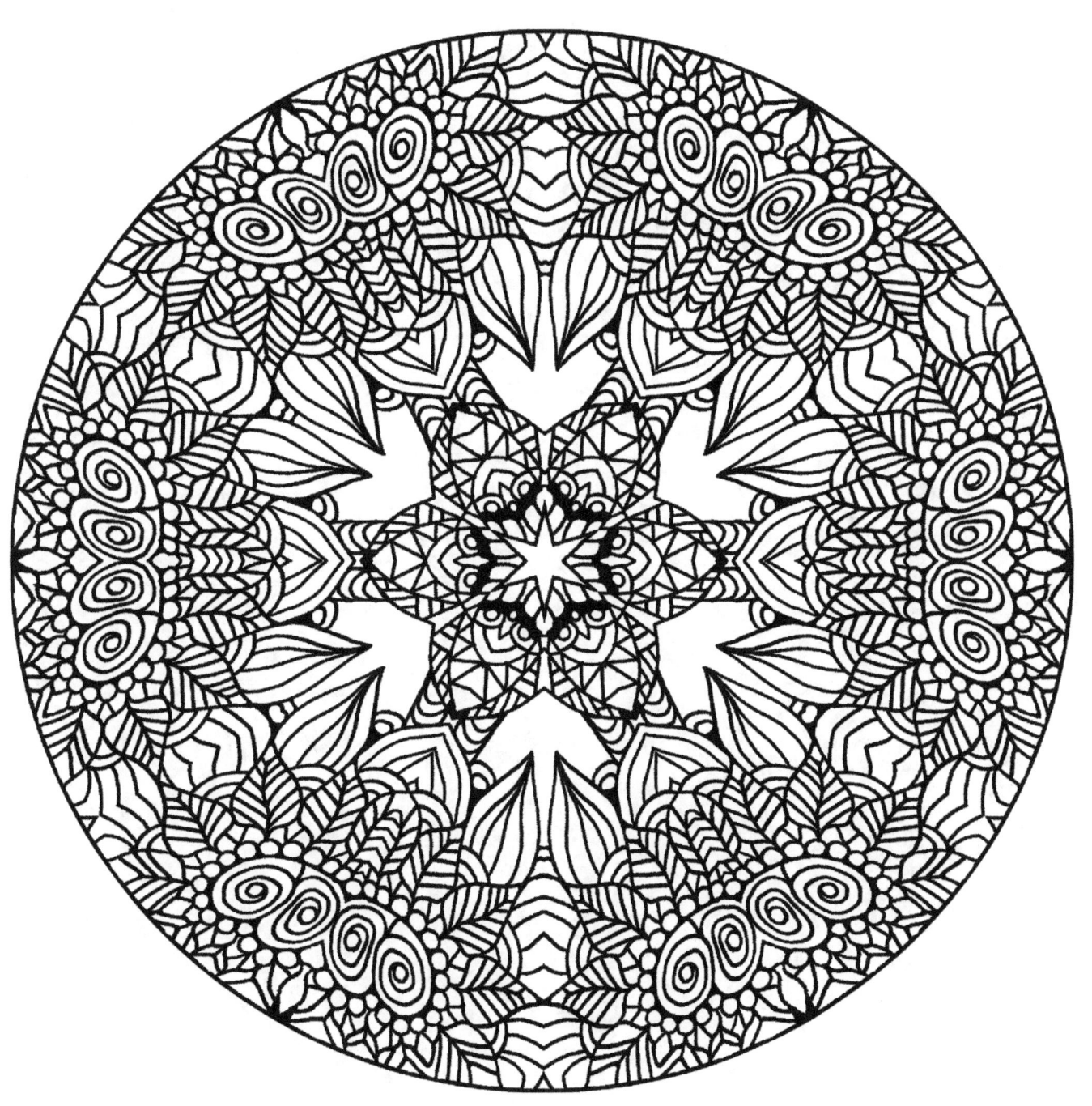

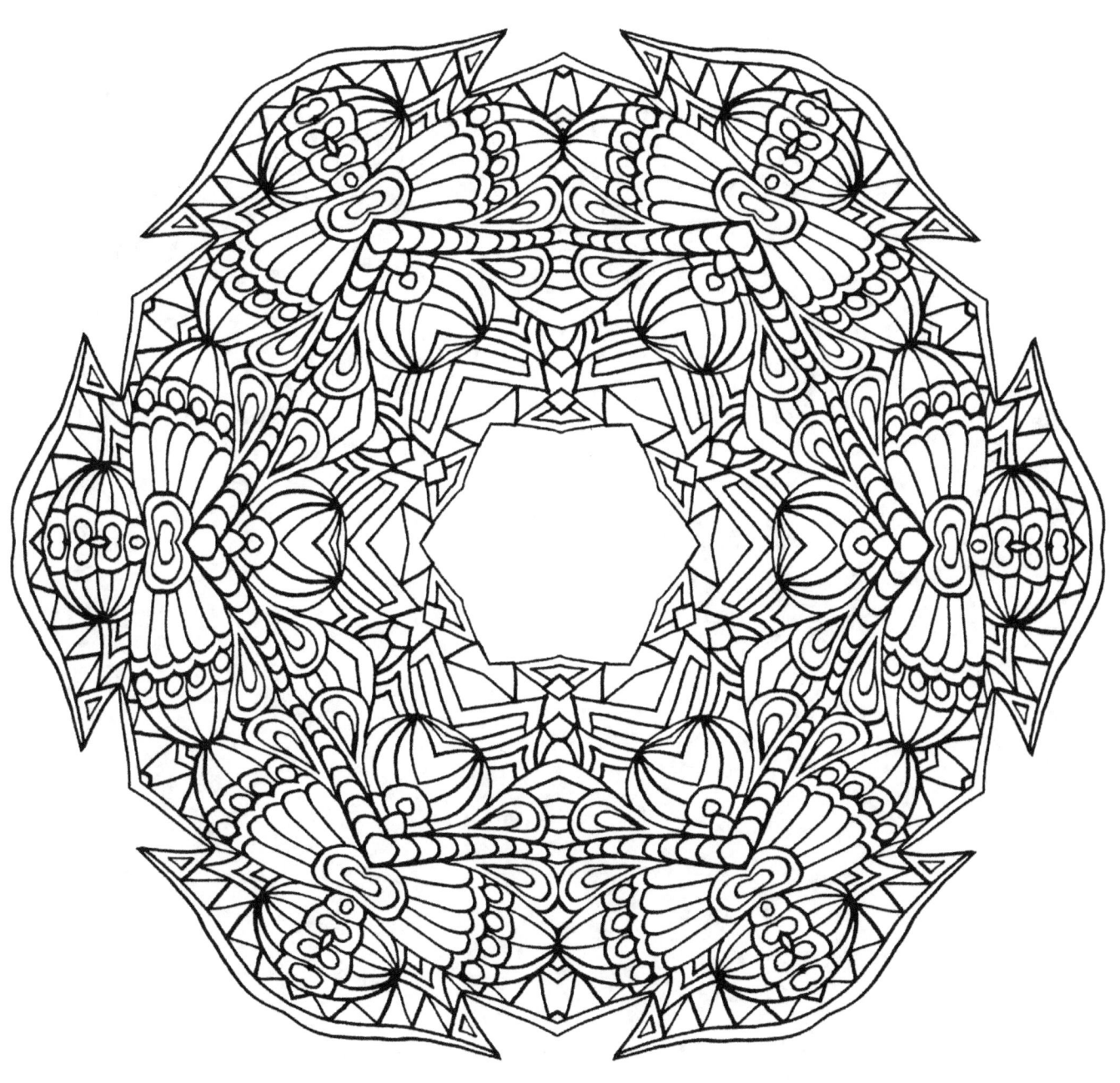

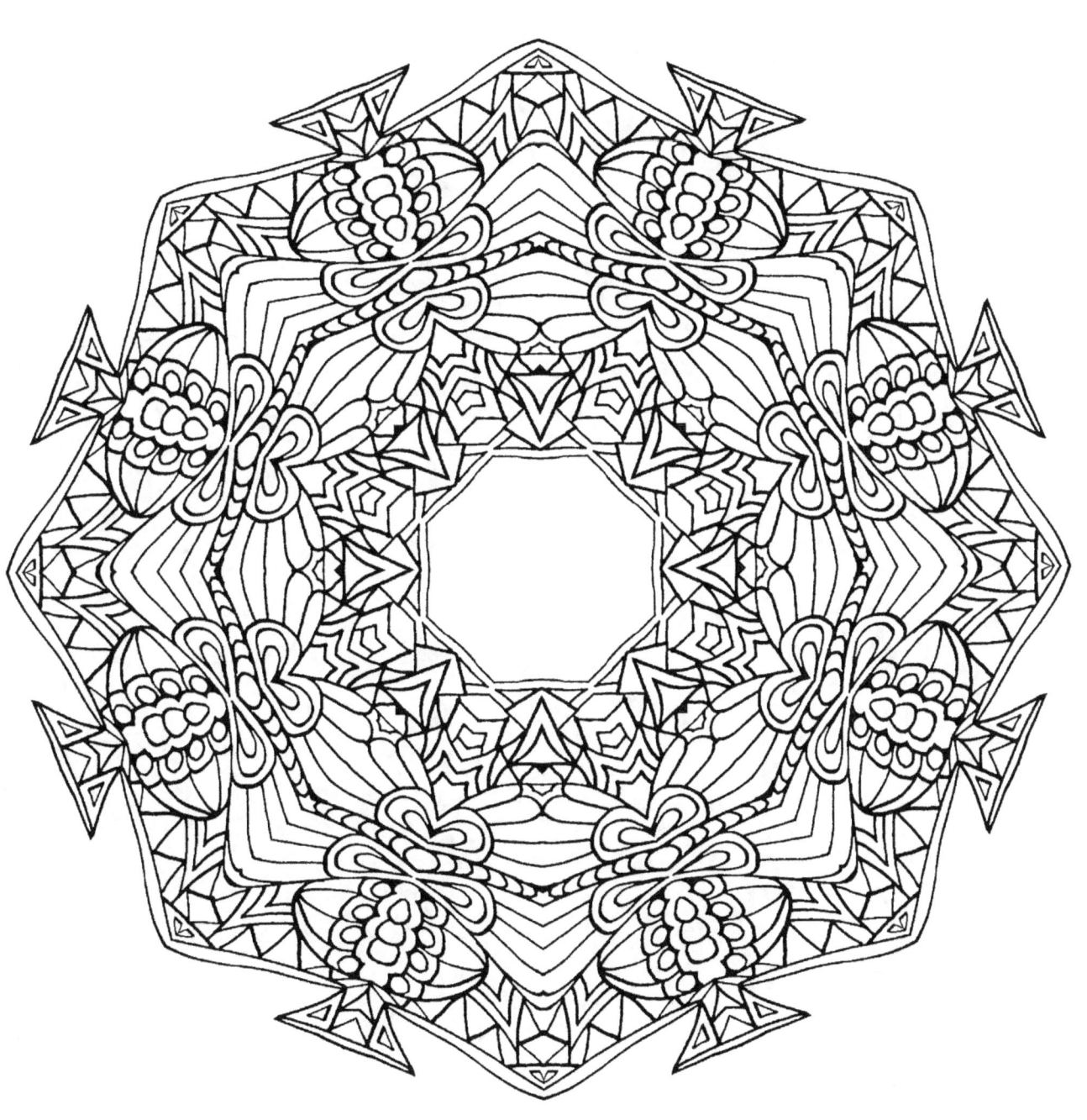

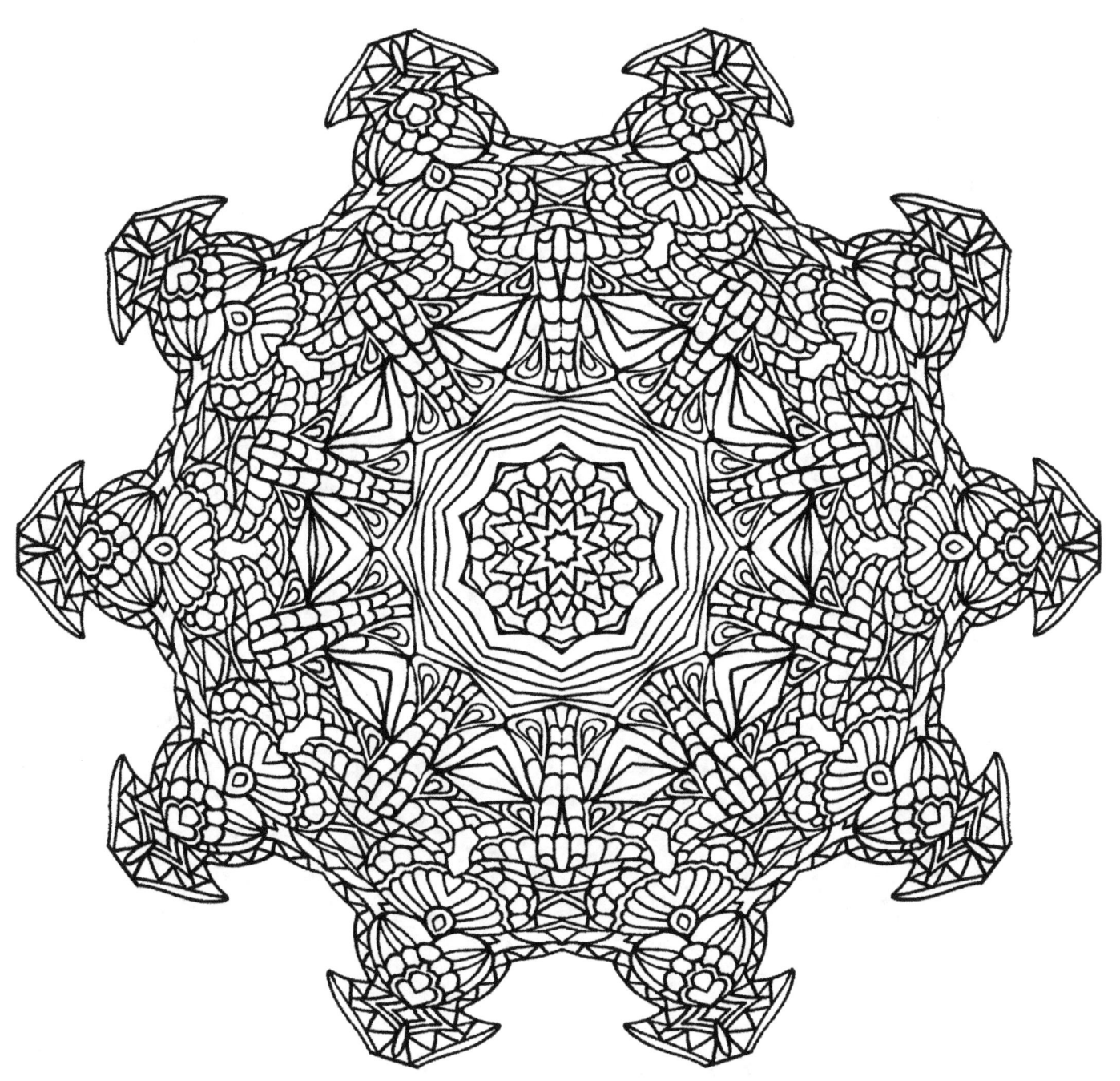

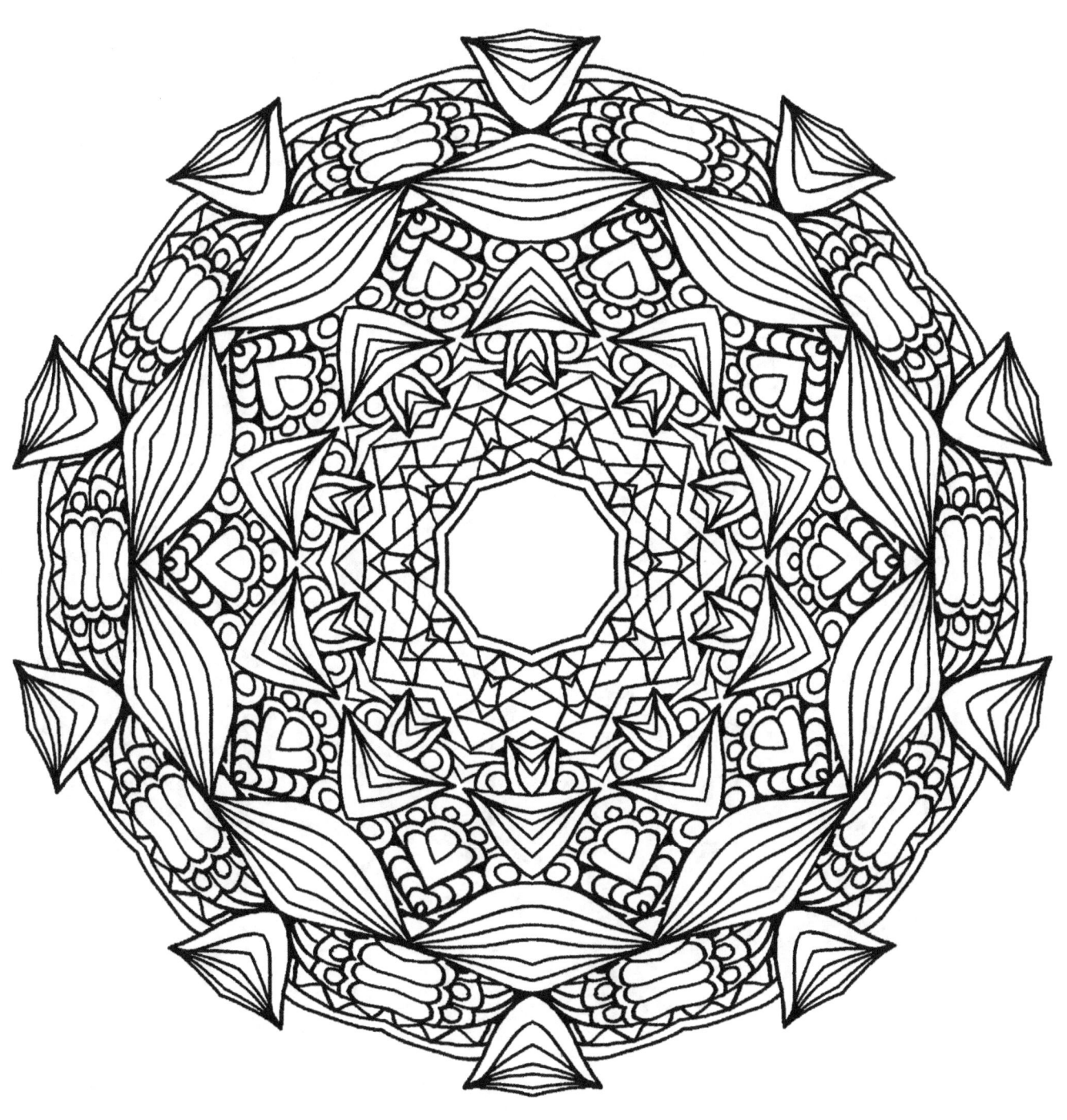

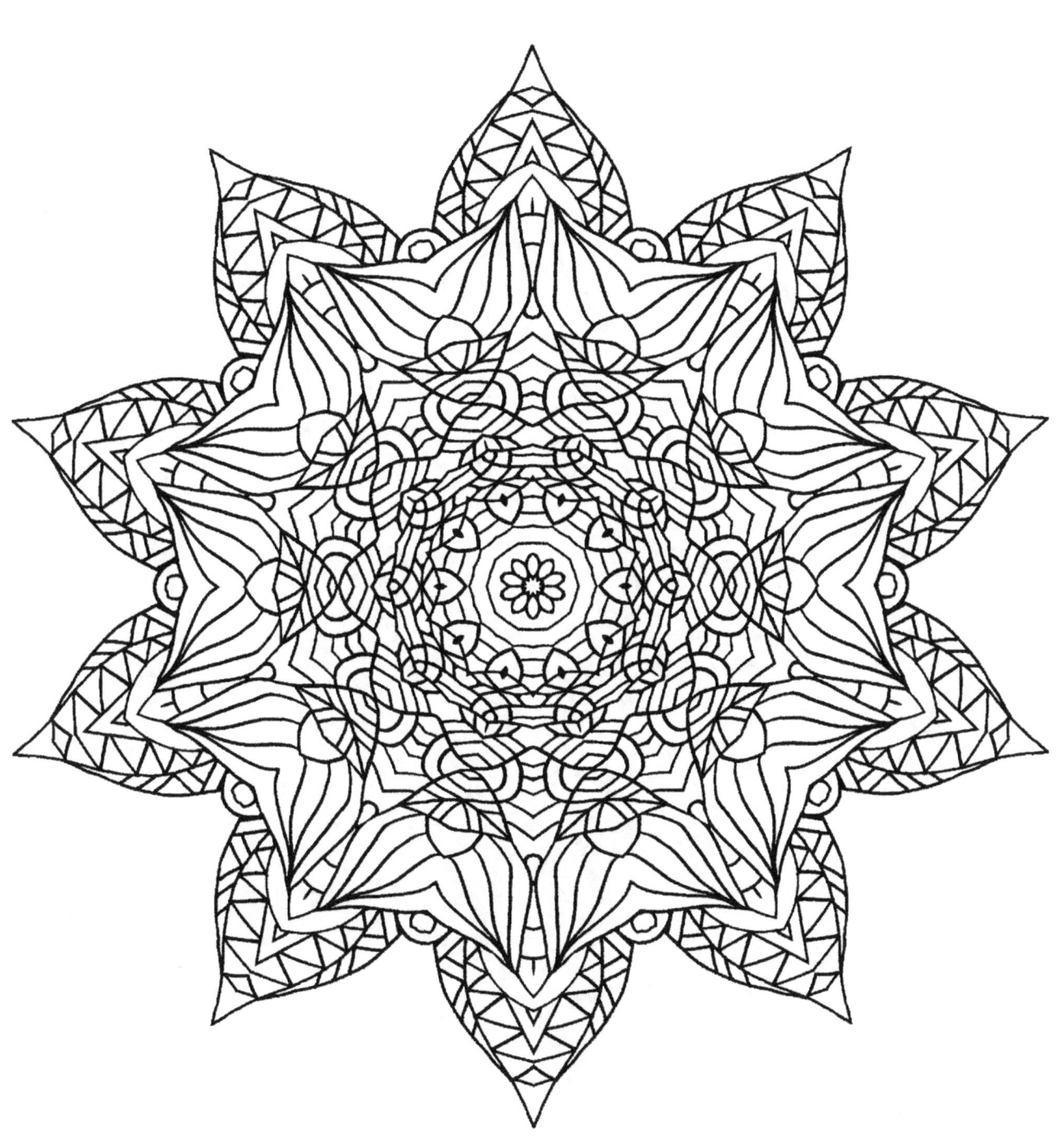

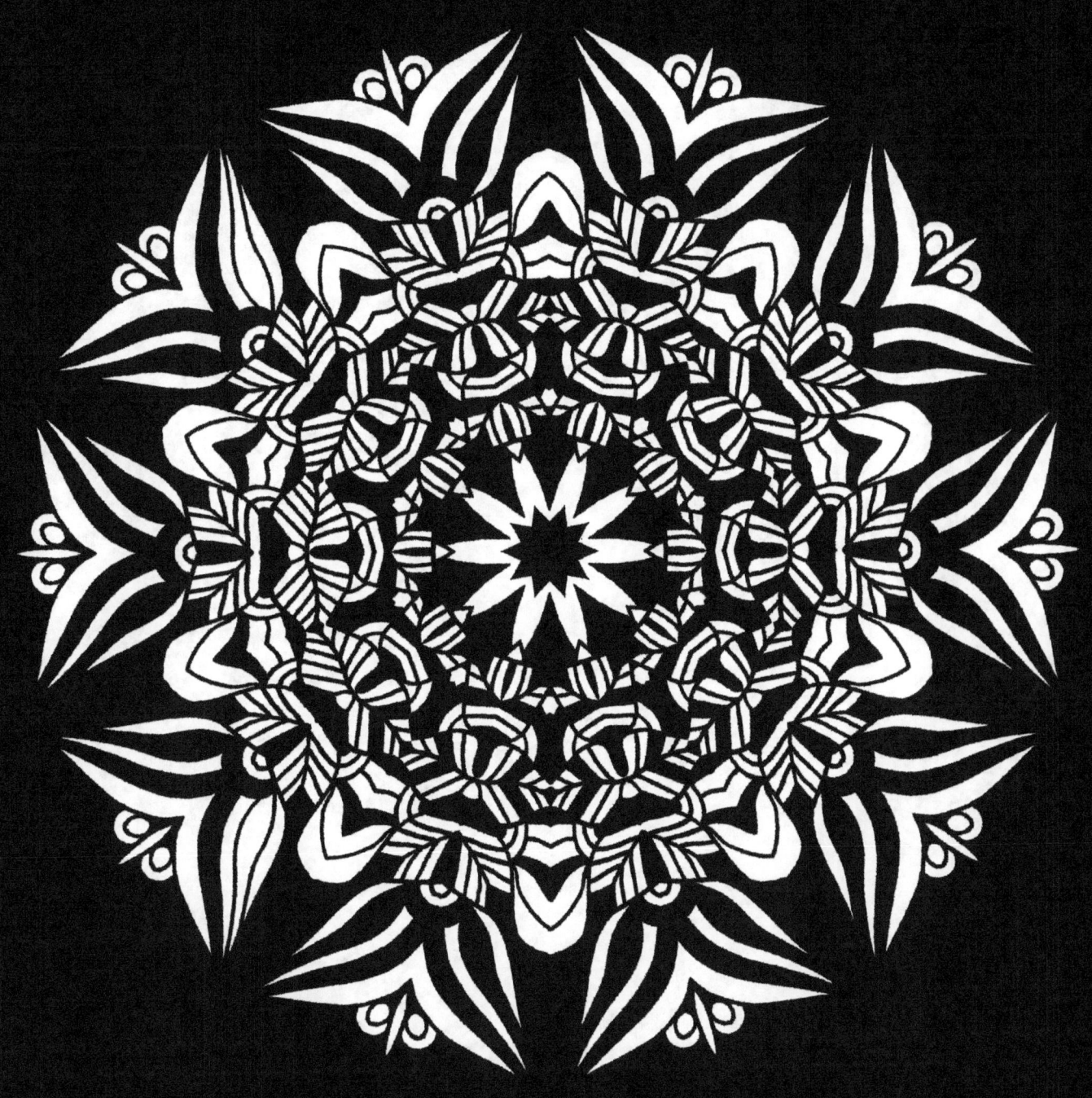

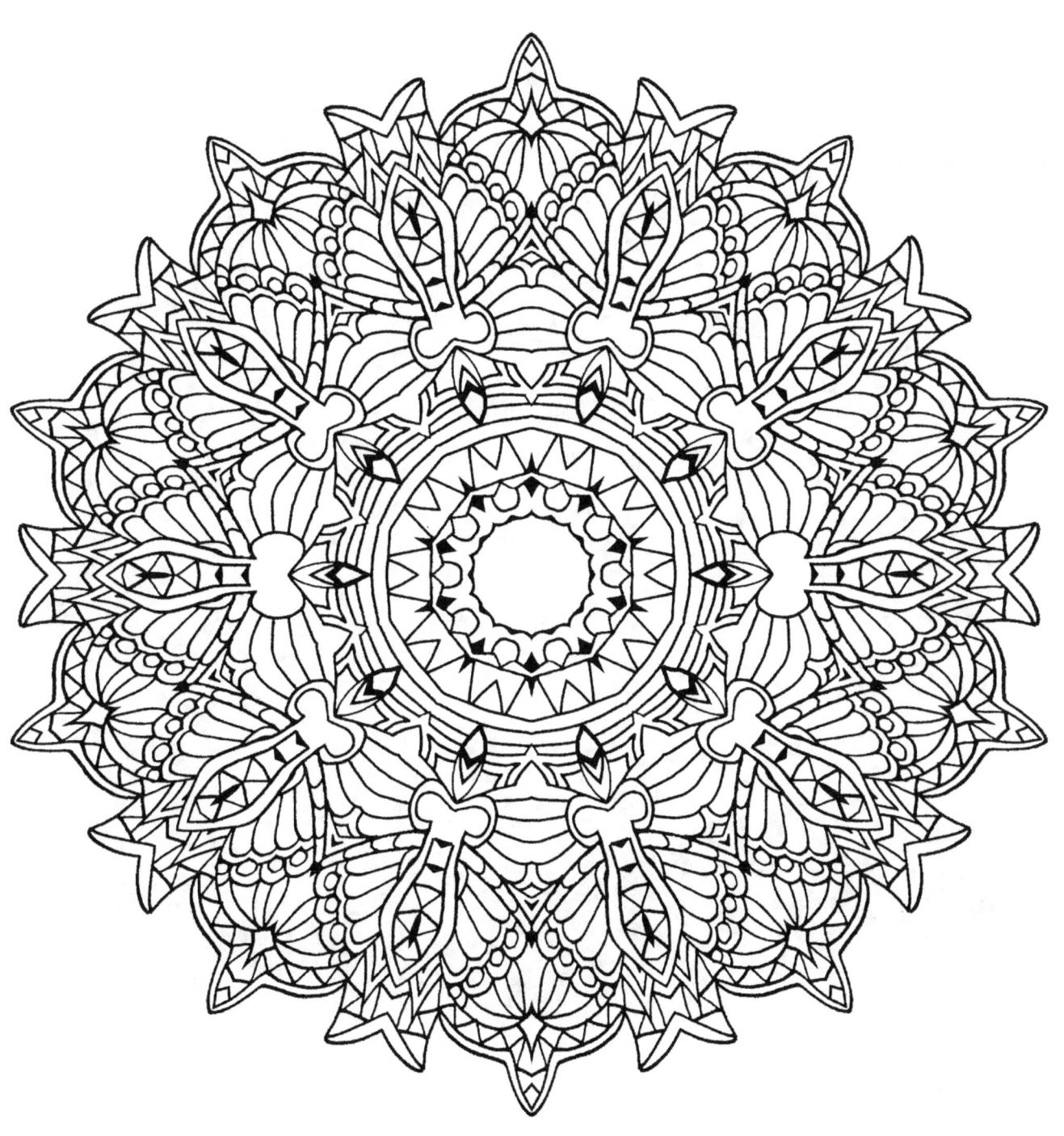

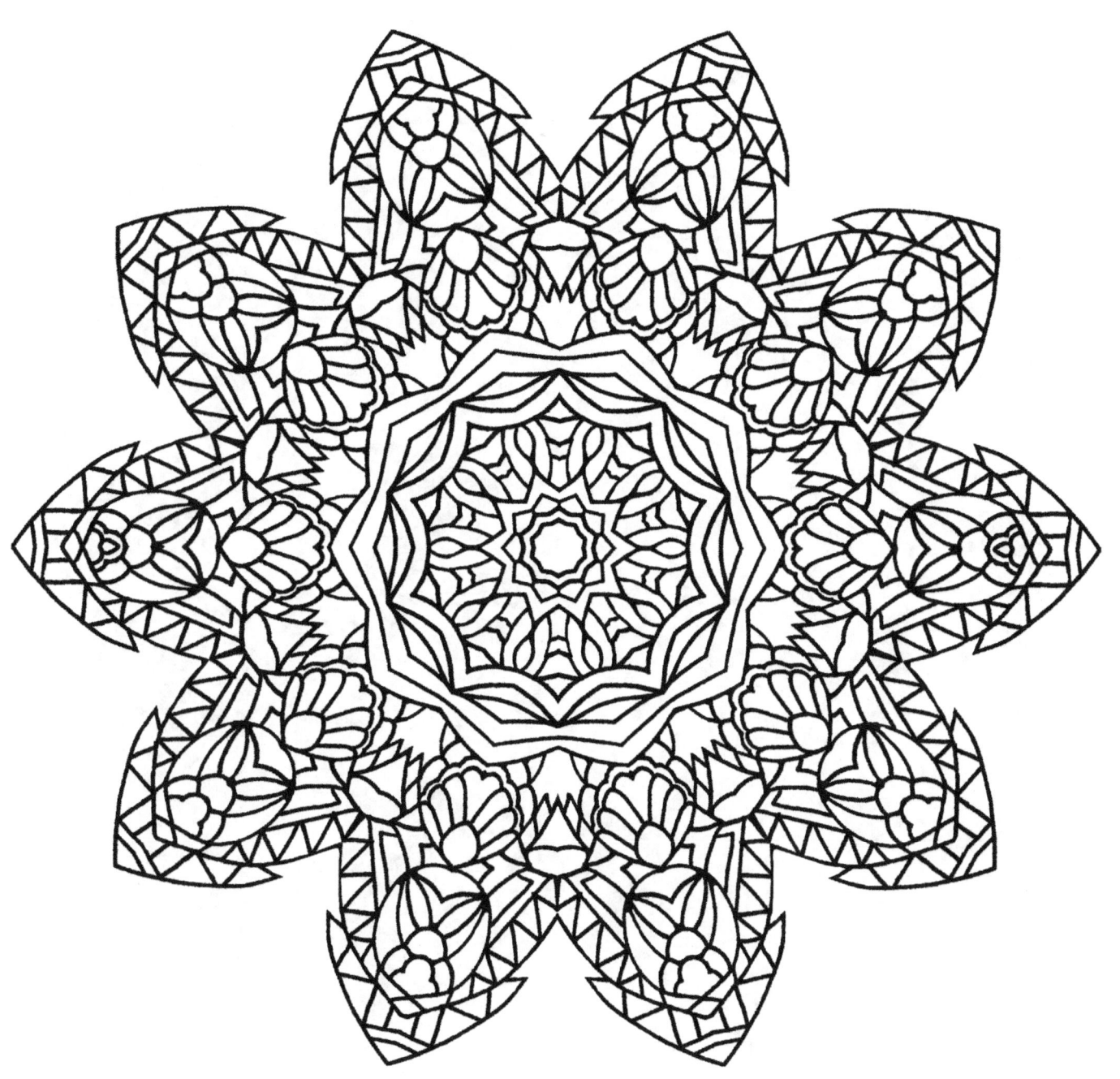

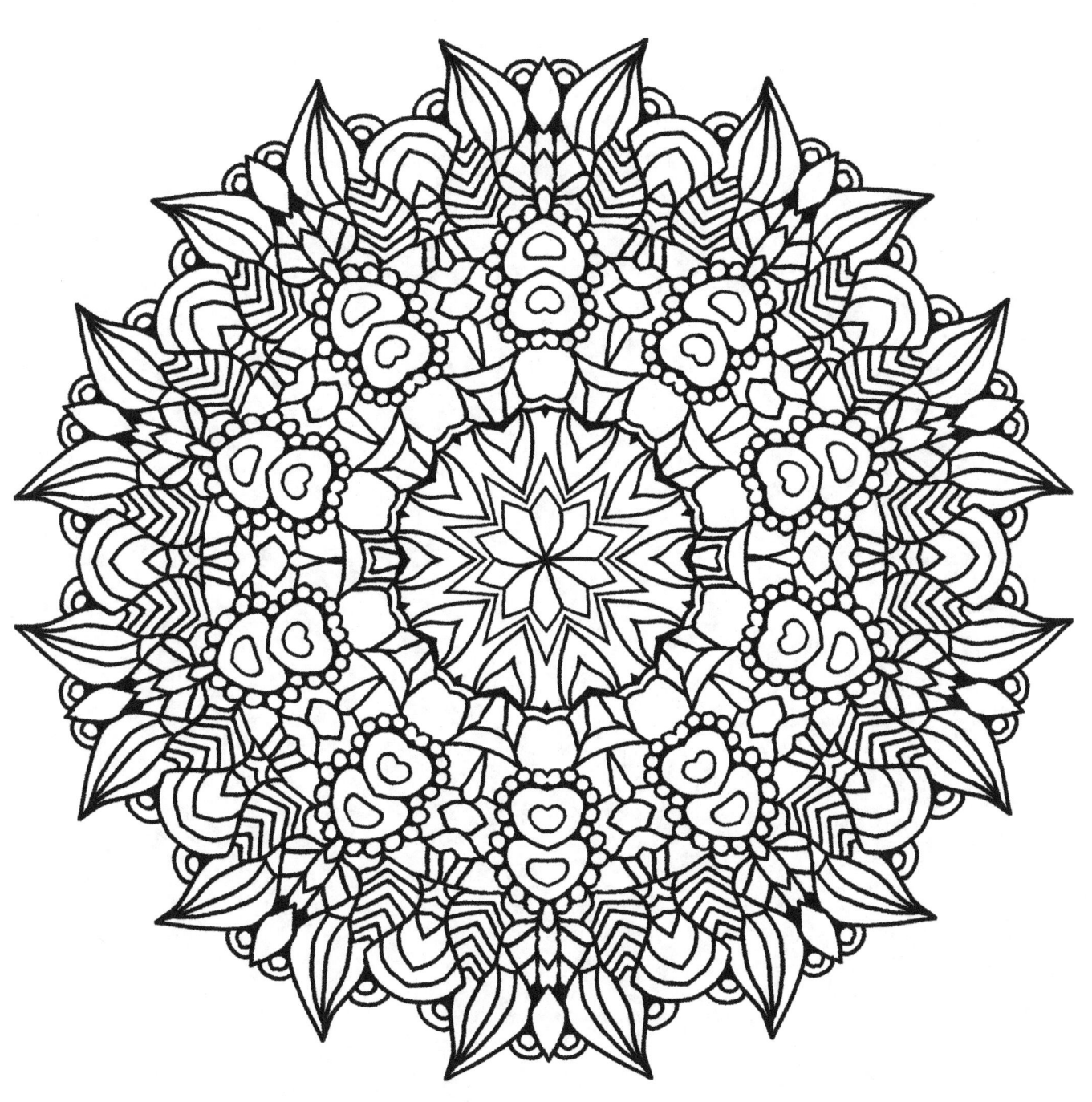

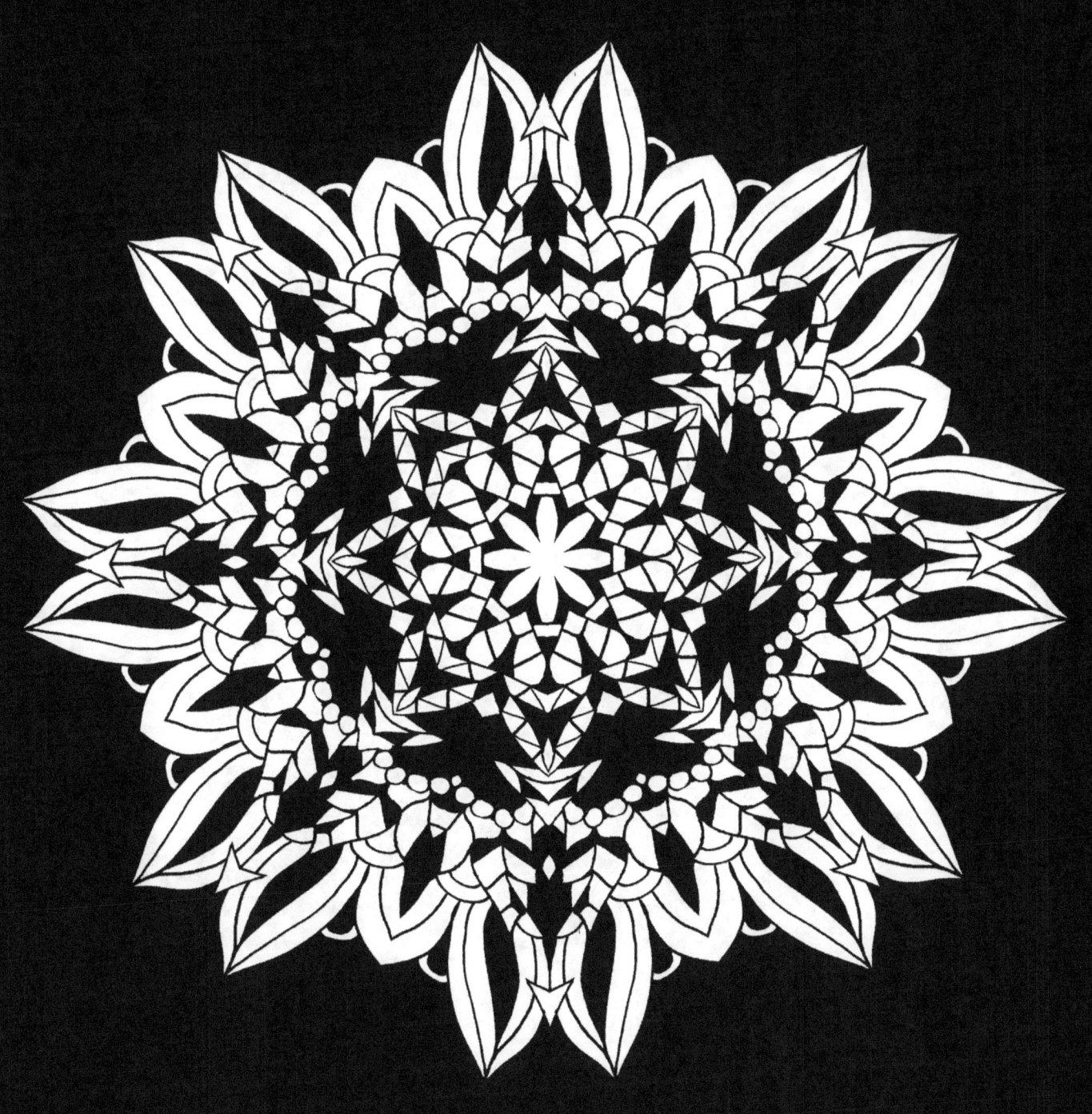

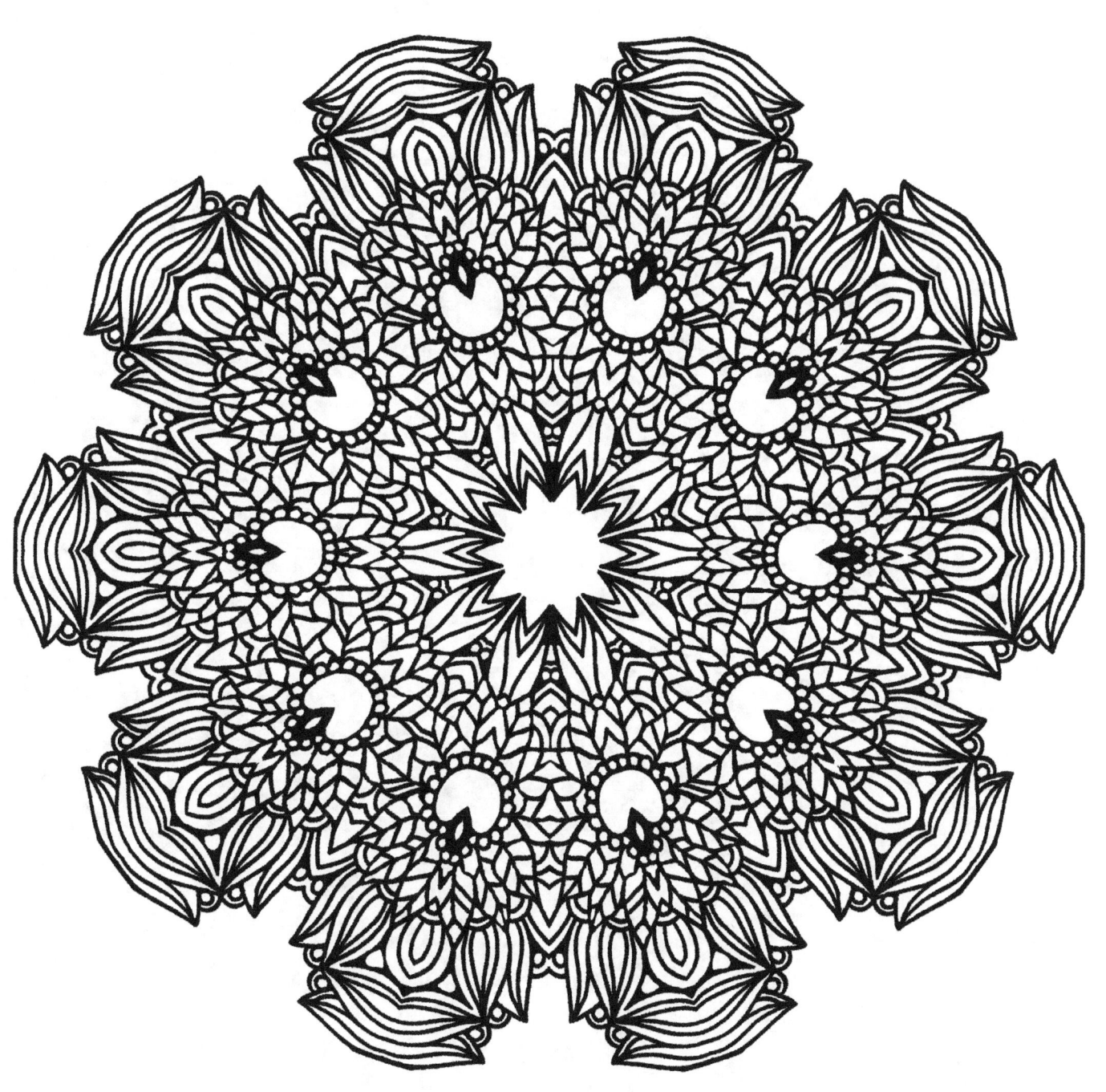

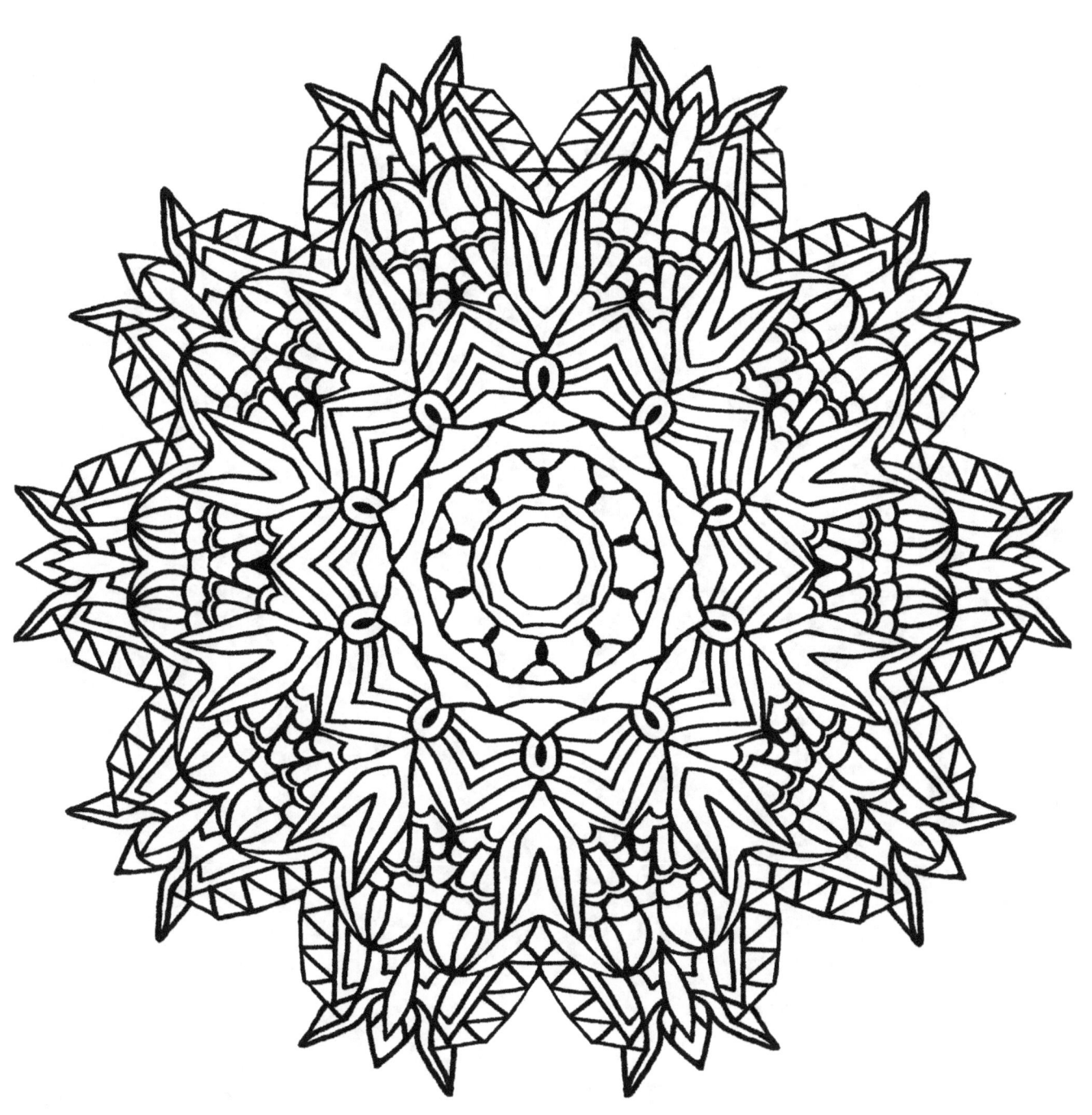

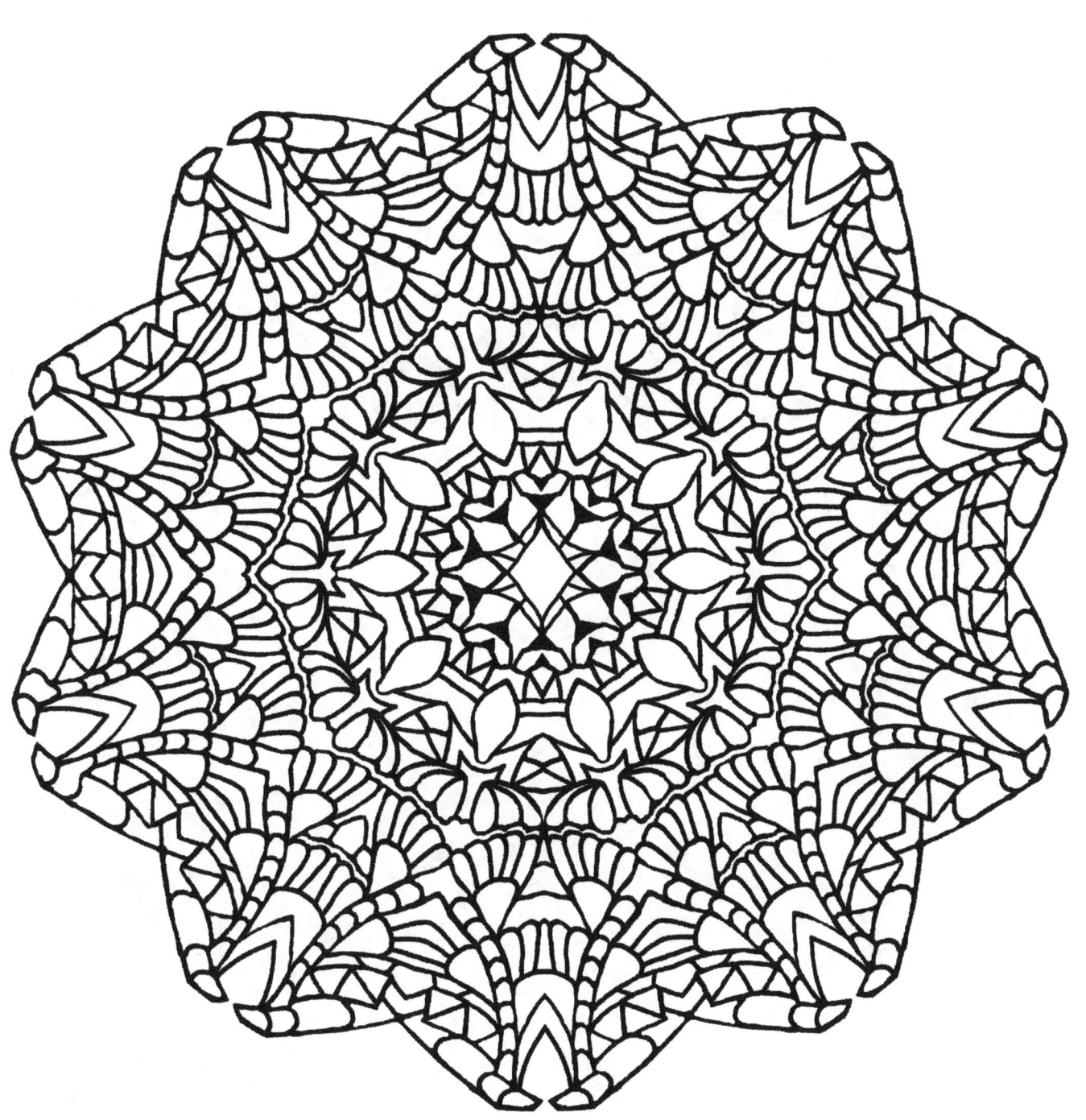

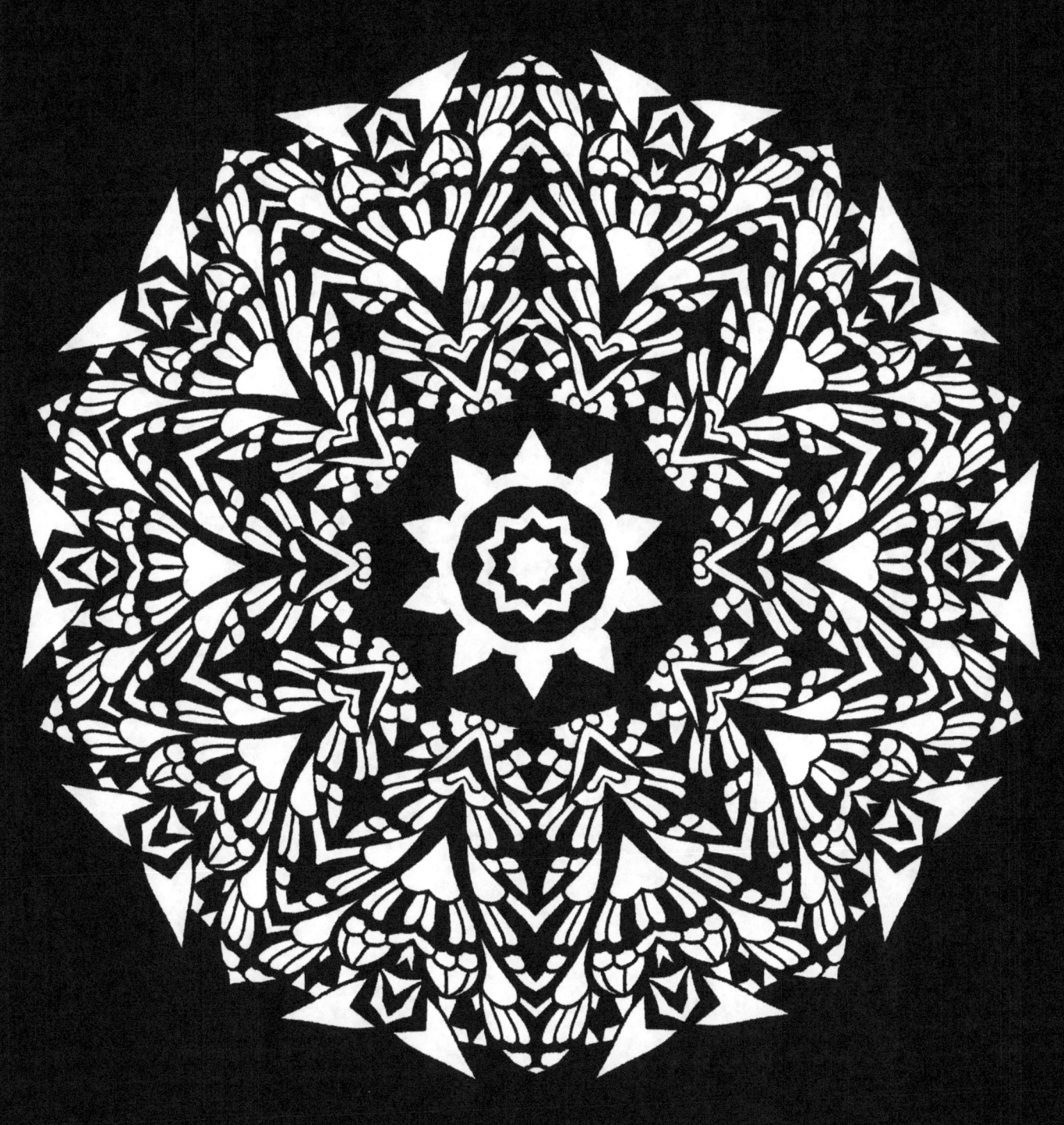

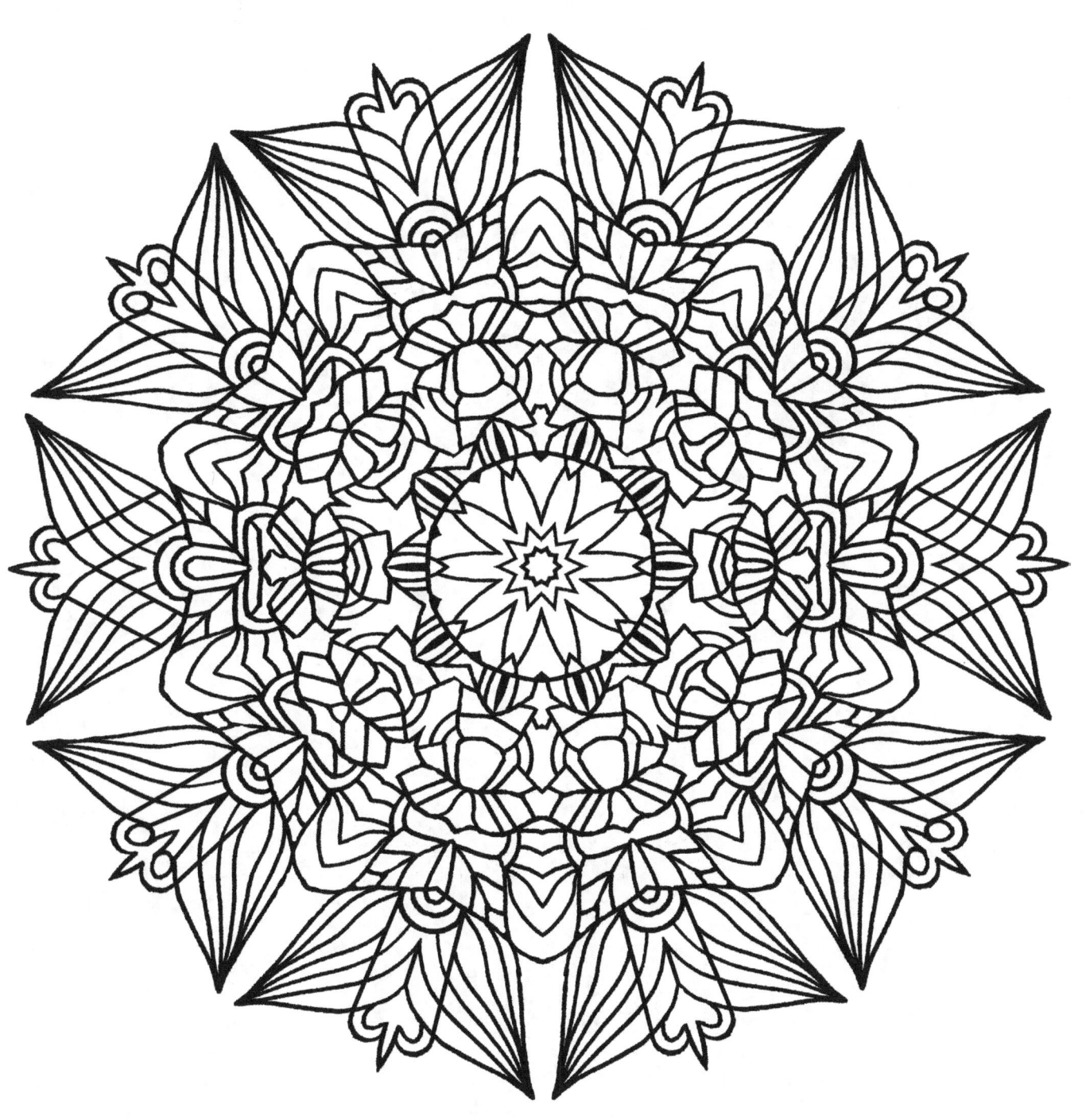

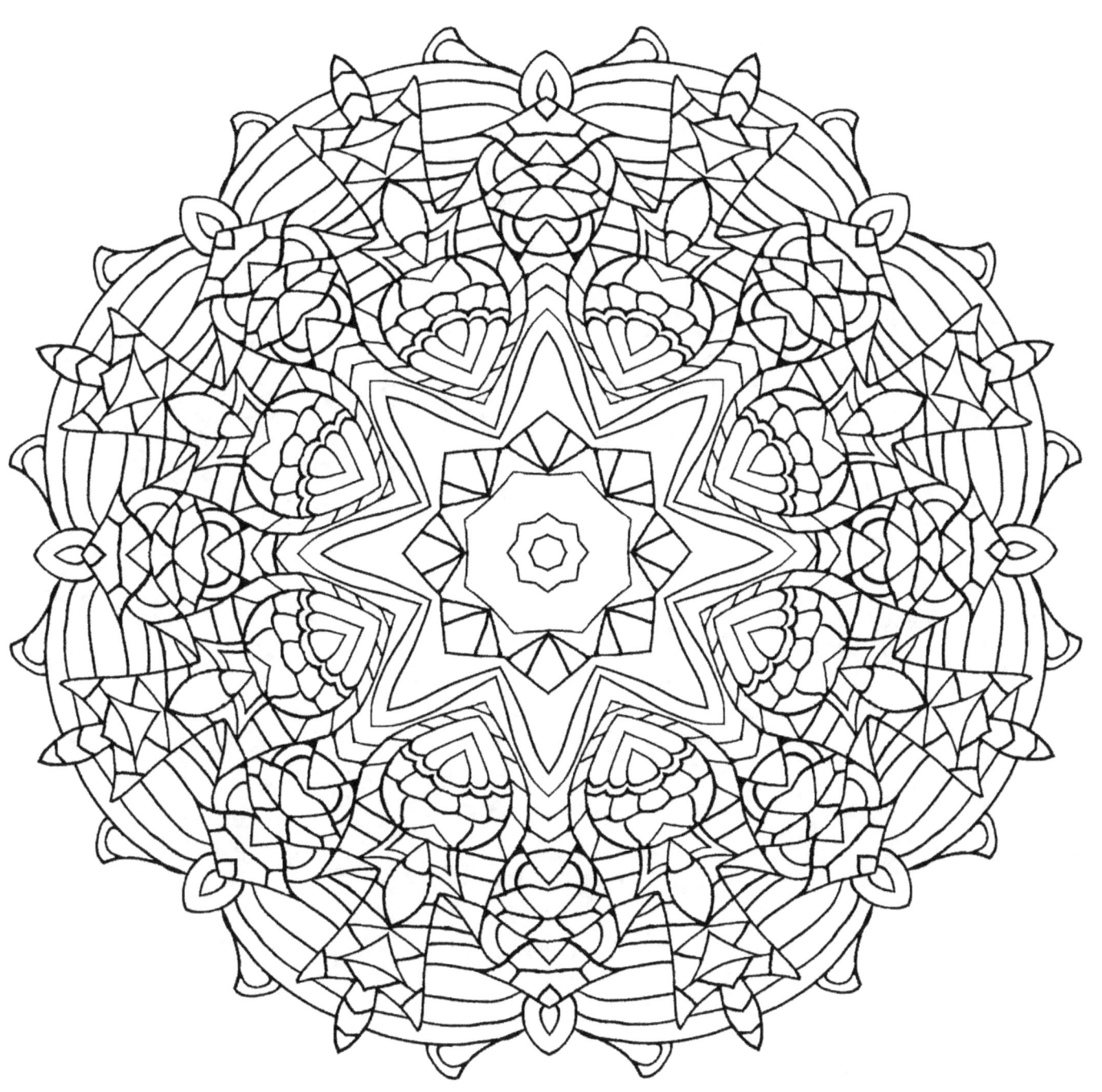

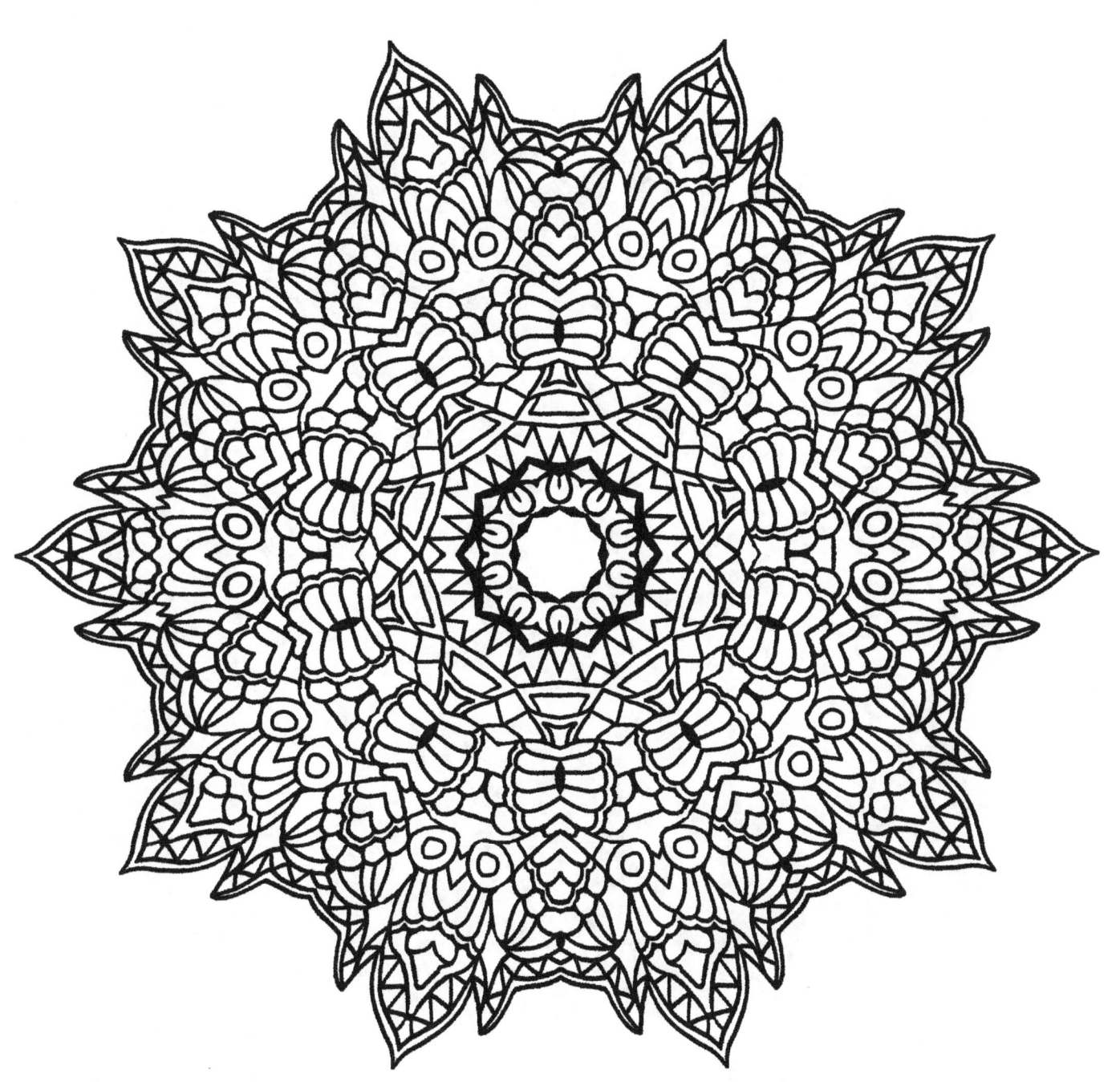

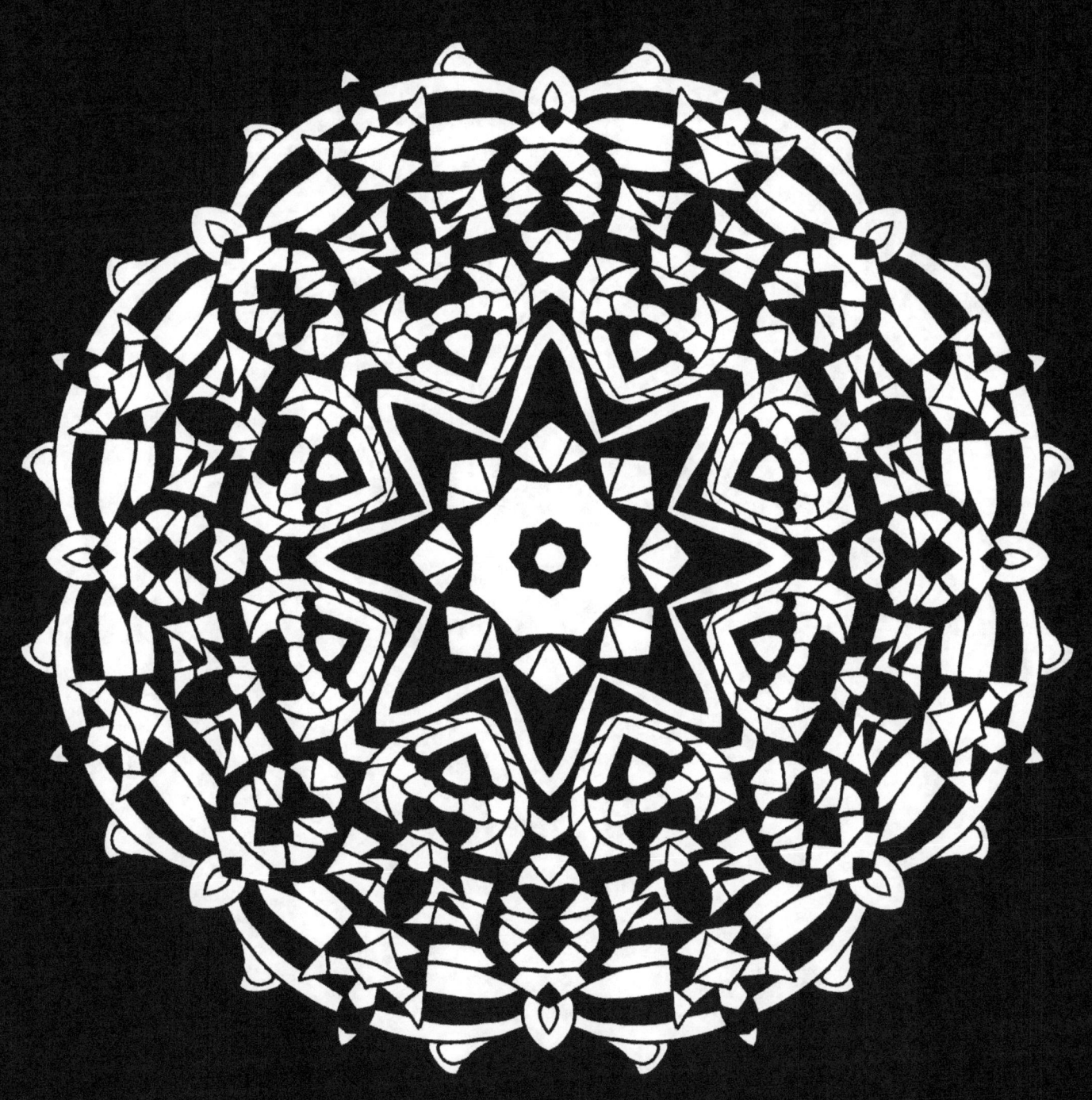

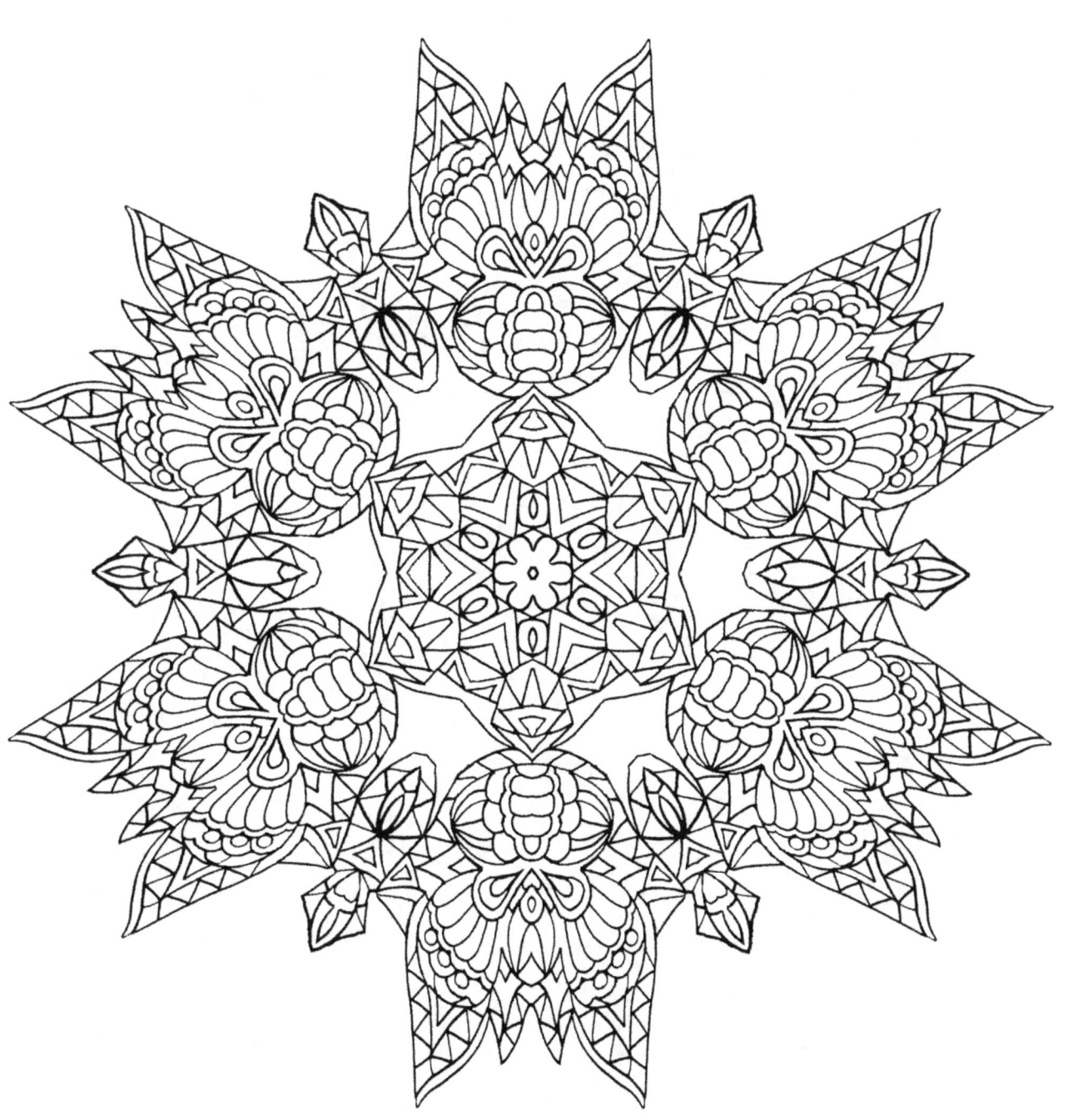

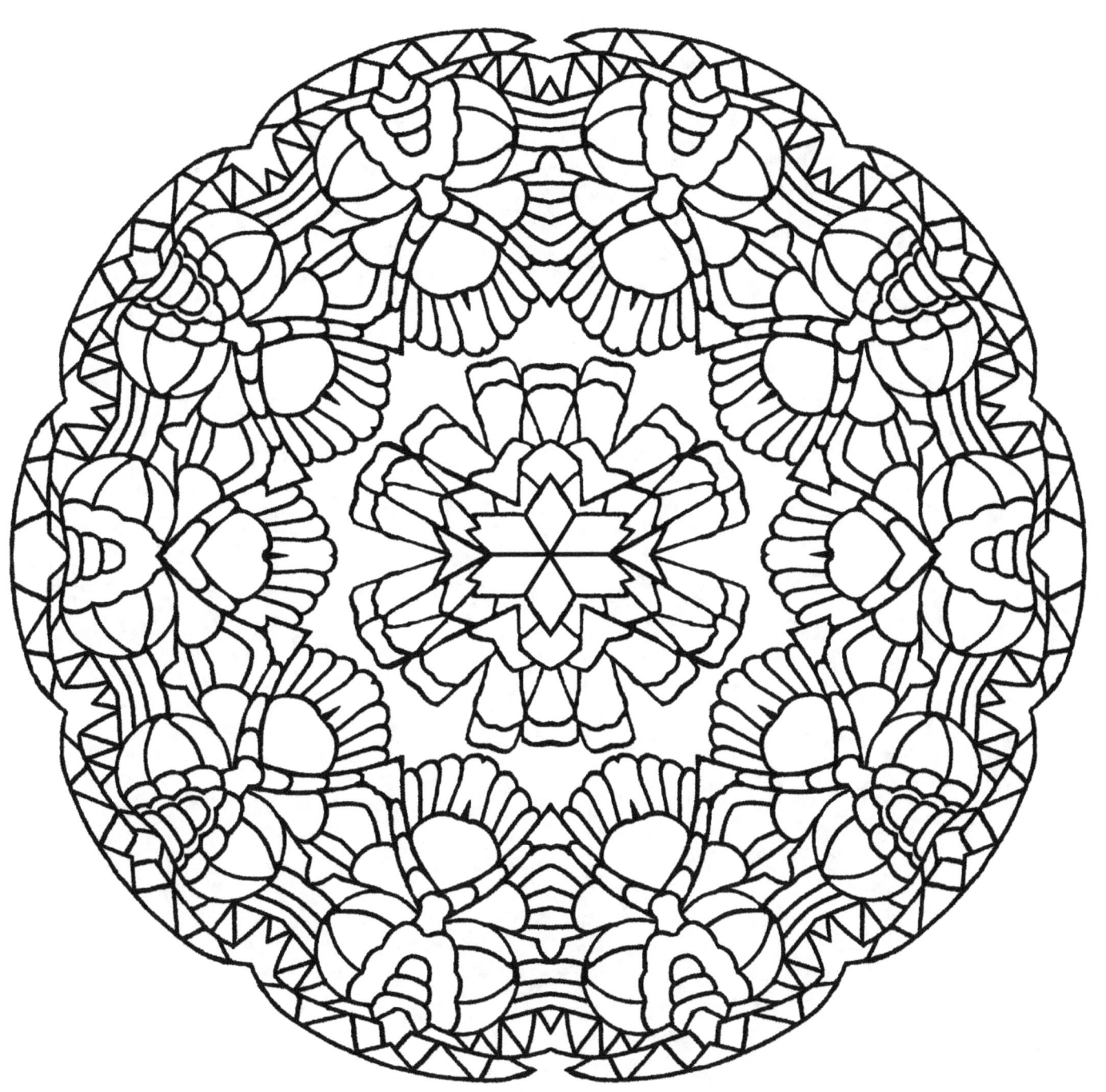

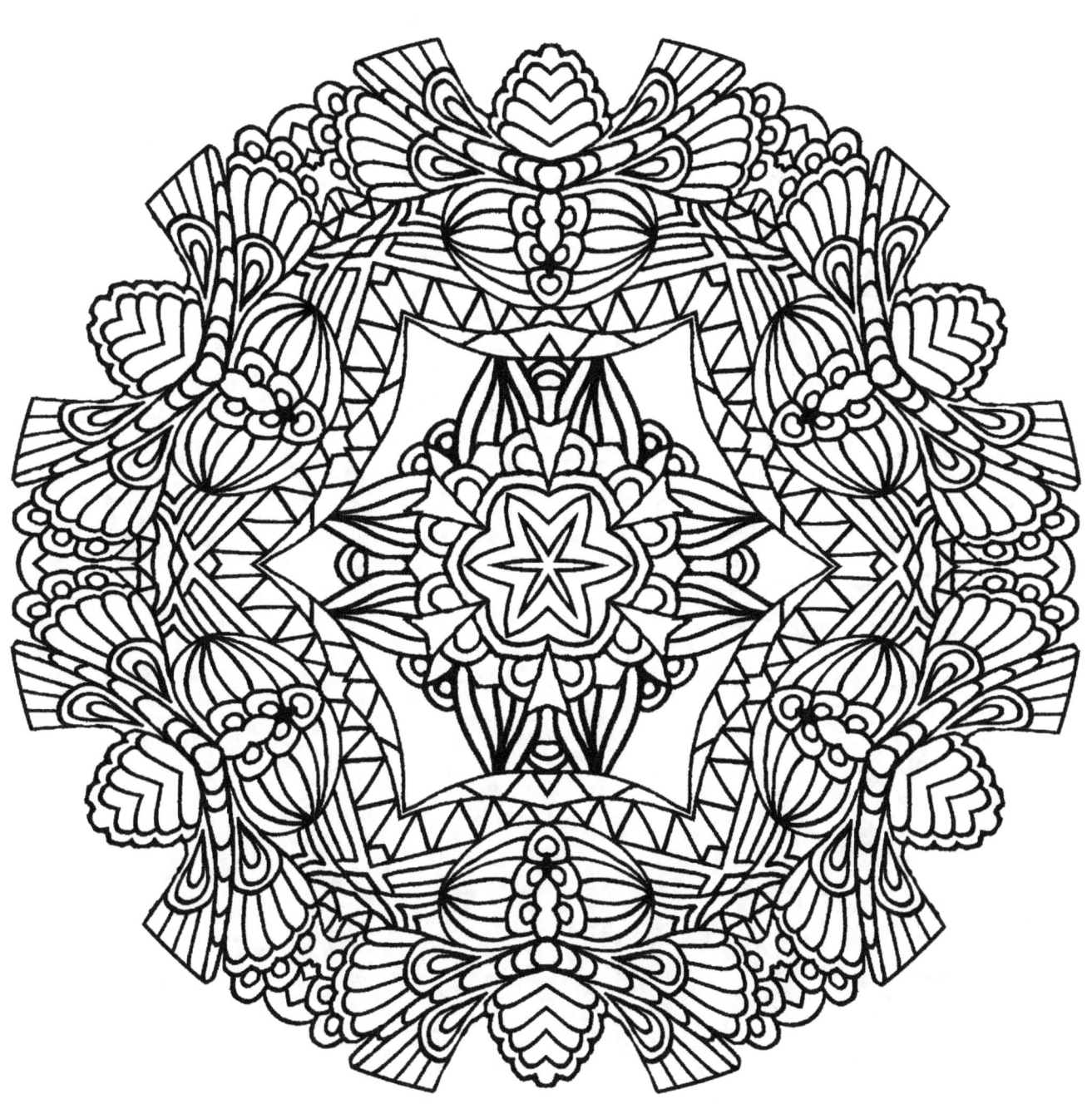

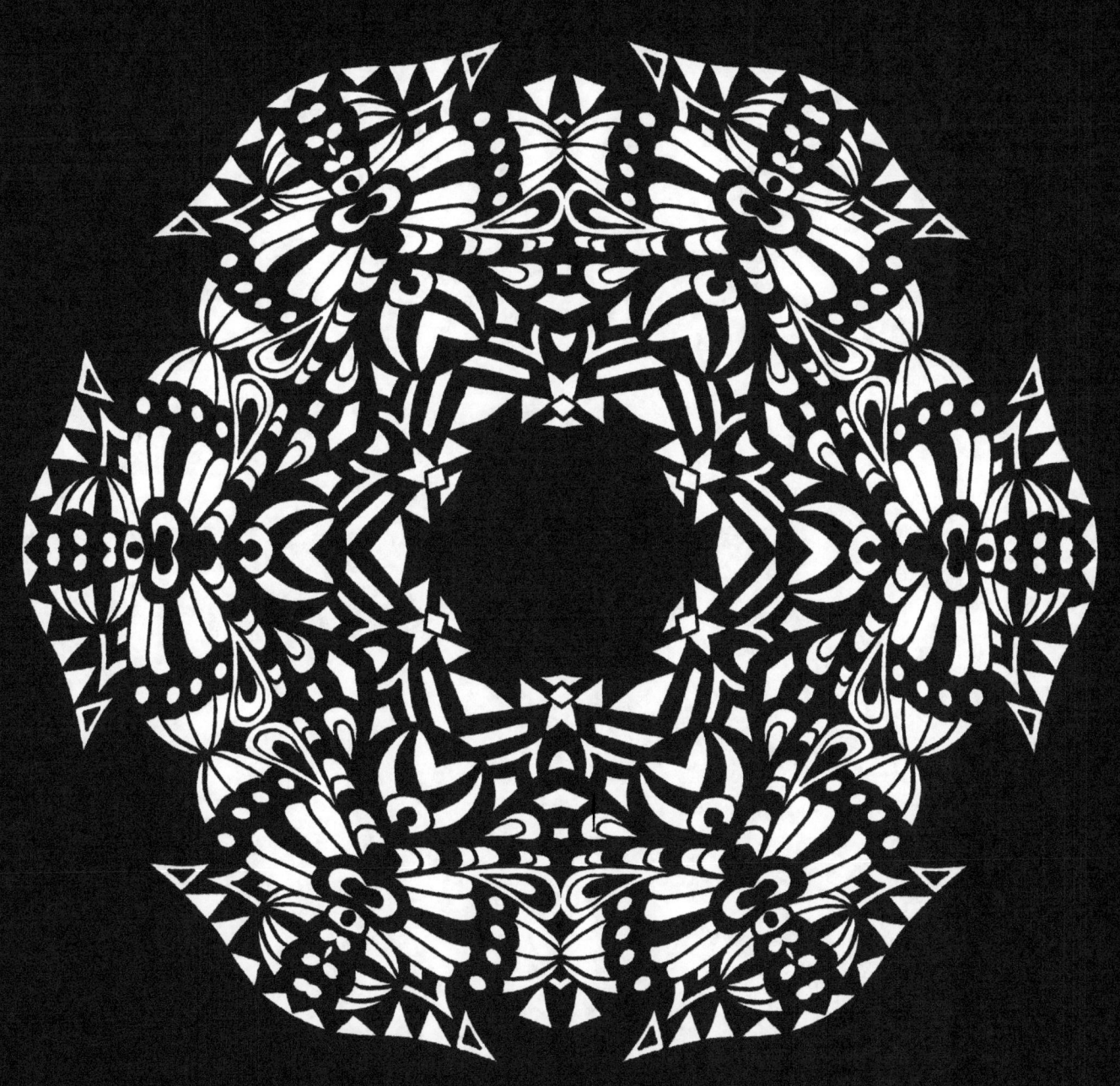

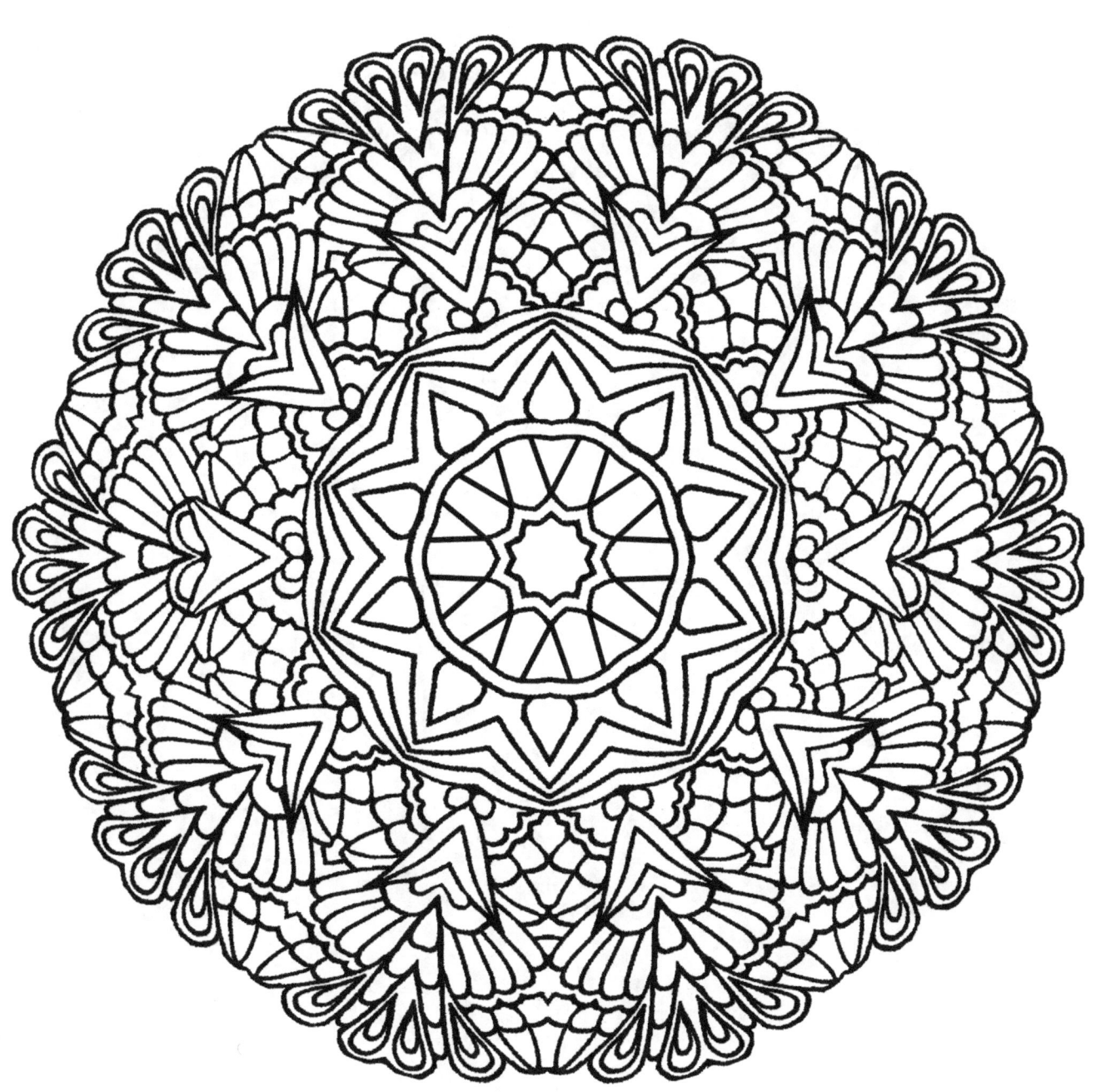

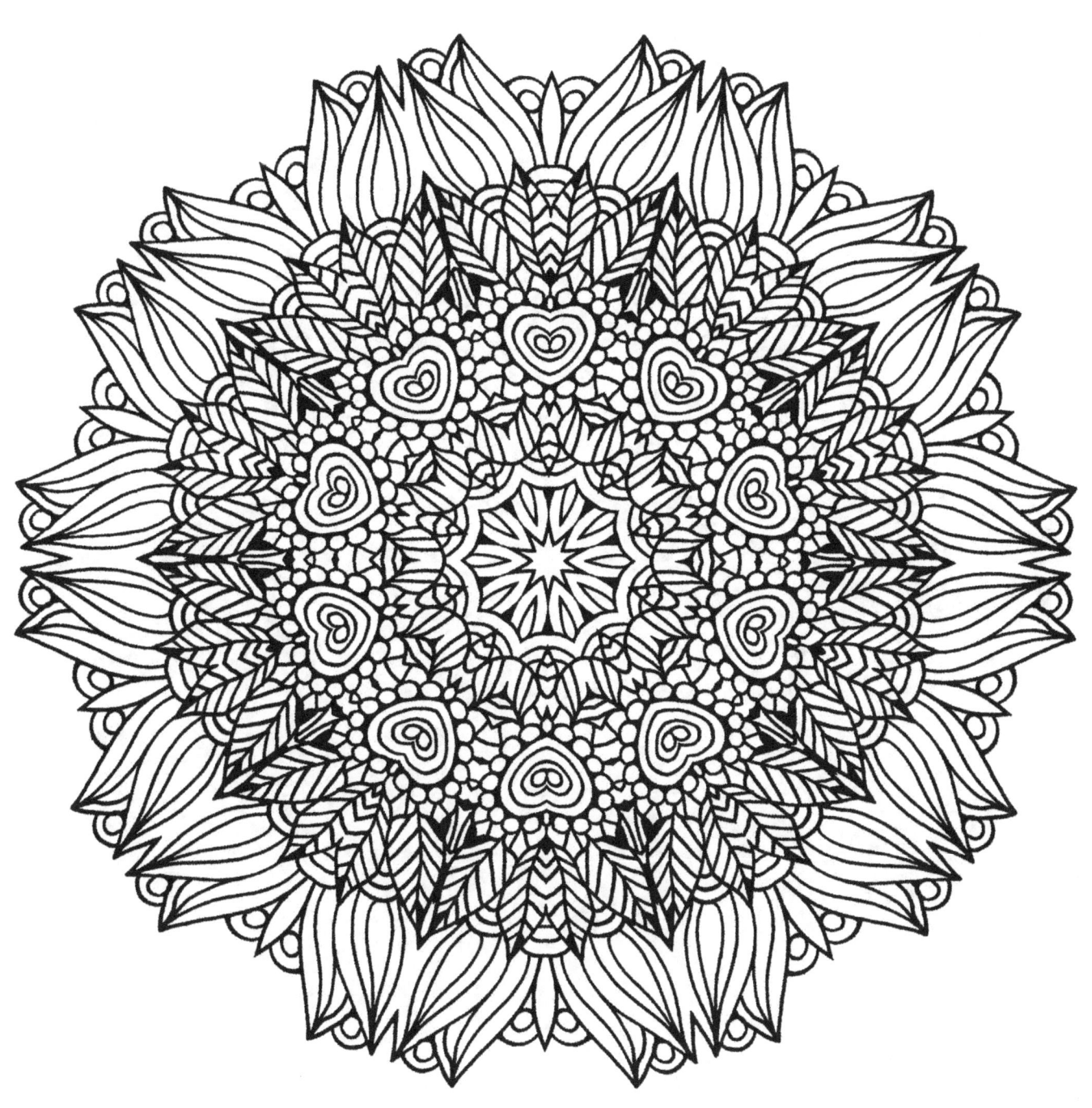

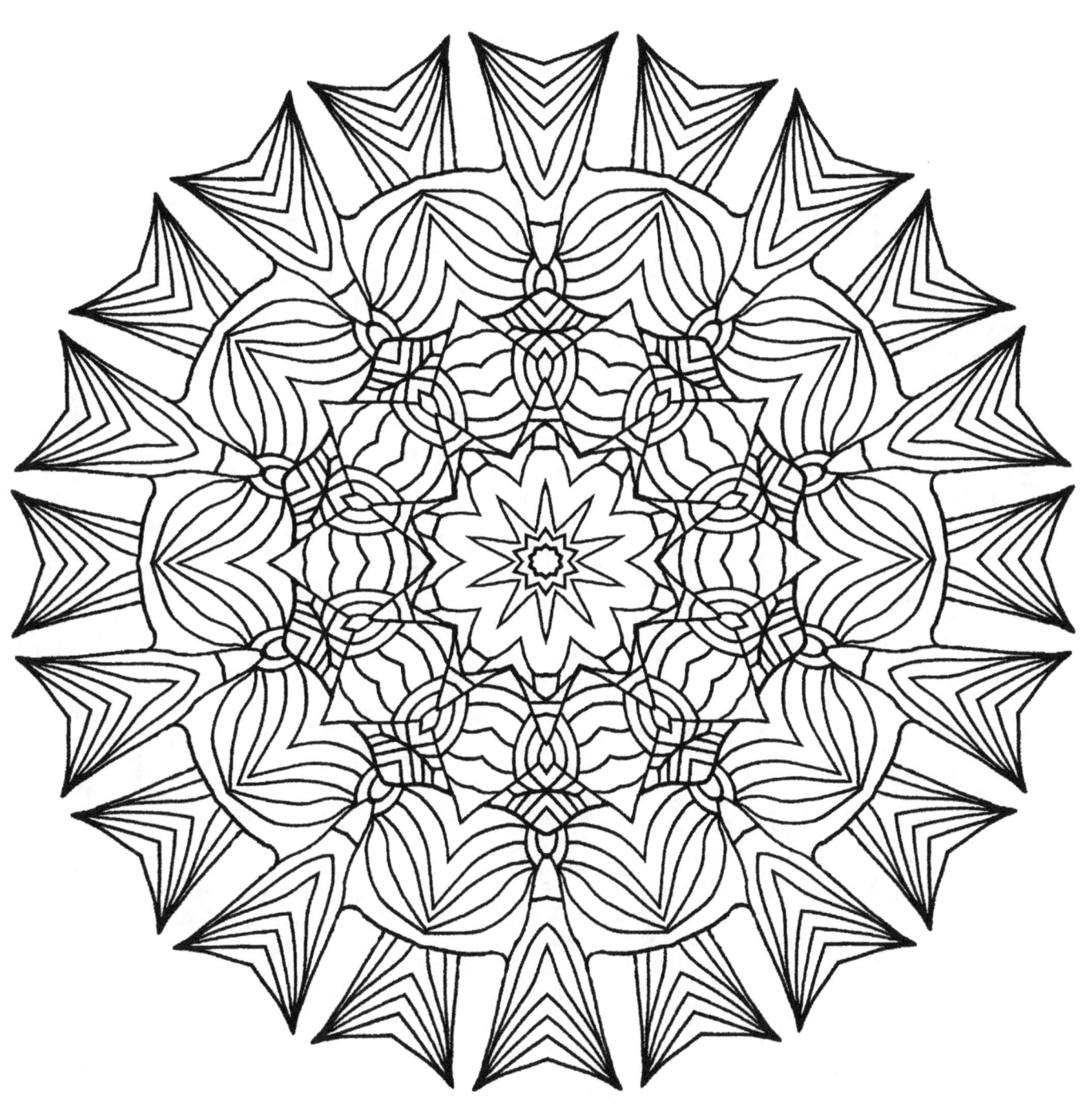

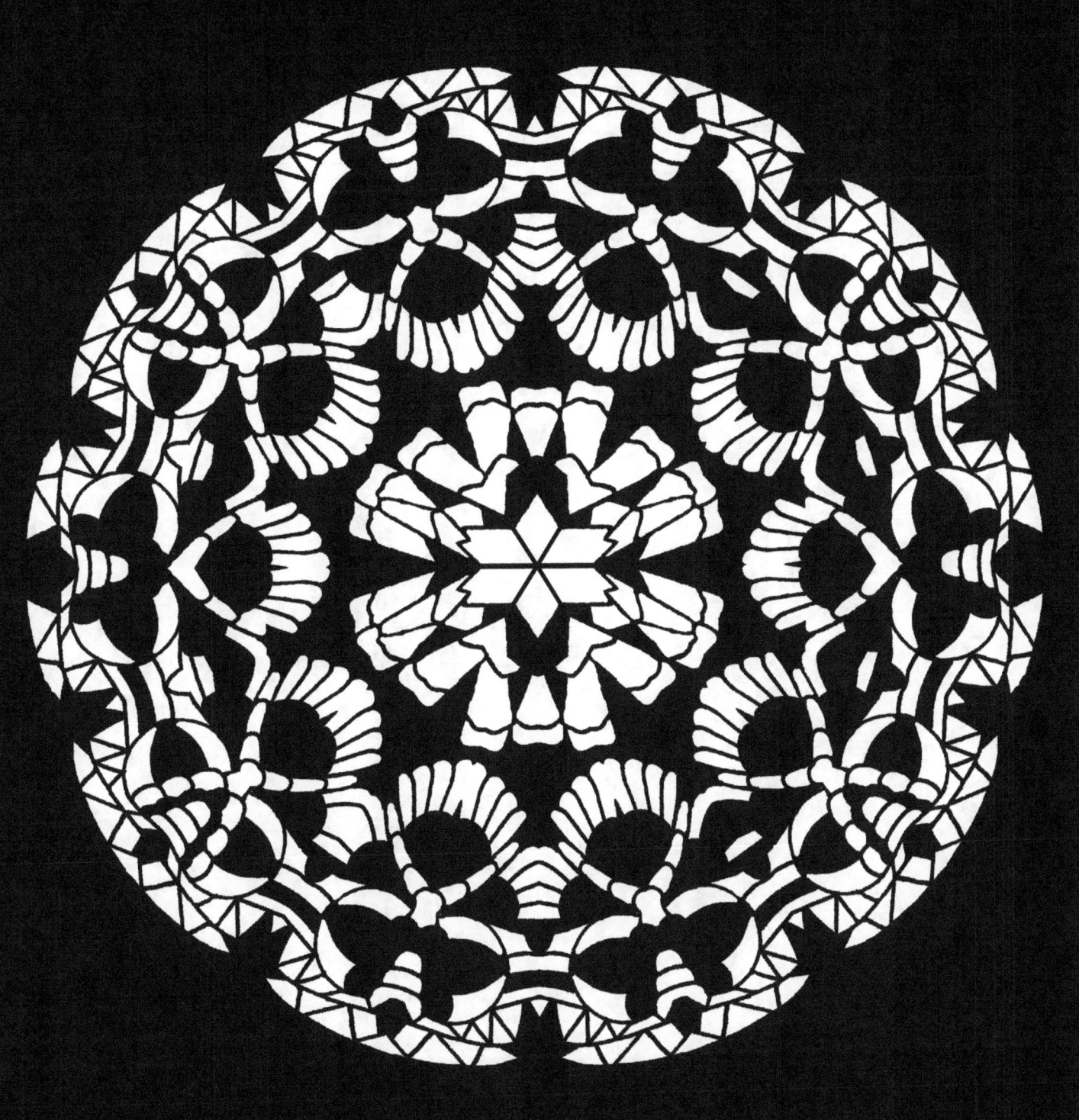

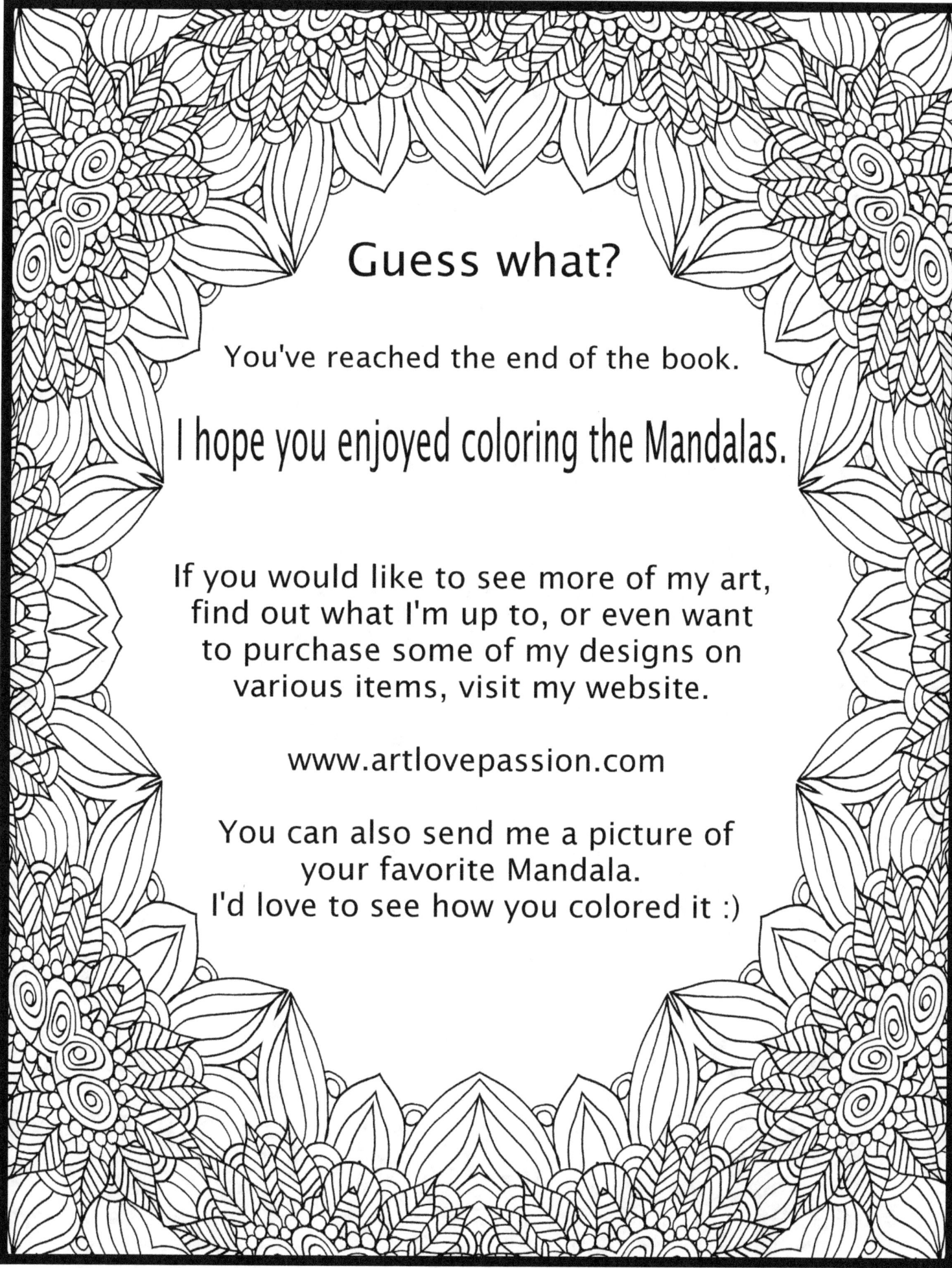

Guess what?

You've reached the end of the book.

I hope you enjoyed coloring the Mandalas.

If you would like to see more of my art, find out what I'm up to, or even want to purchase some of my designs on various items, visit my website.

www.artlovepassion.com

You can also send me a picture of your favorite Mandala.
I'd love to see how you colored it :)

www.ingramcontent.com/pod-product-compliance
Lightning Source LLC
Chambersburg PA
CBHW080948170526
45158CB00008B/2408

* 9 7 8 0 6 9 2 5 2 0 8 9 5 *